WAKE UP AMERICA,

IT'S TIME TO REPENT

WAKE UP AMERICA,
IT'S TIME TO REPENT

J.B. LIGHT

JBL BOOK PUBLISHING

PHOENIX, ARIZONA

WAKE UP AMERICA,
IT'S TIME TO REPENT

Published by JBL Book Publishing
Phoenix, Arizona

J.B. Light, Publisher / Editorial Director
Yvonne Rose/Quality Press.info, Book Packager

Paperback ISBN #: 978-1-0878-6903-2
Ebook ISBN #: 978-1-0878-7069-4
Library of Congress Control Number: 2022907661

Dedication

This book is dedicated to all of my brothers and sisters
of the Lord whether hued still or have hueloss for the sake
of coming together in healing of minds, changes in attitudes
and beliefs, and doing what is most pleasing to our Lord that
we say we believe in and on and have chosen to serve.

Acknowledgements

To our Lord for speaking the words to me to write
for the edification of His body of believers.
To my family who gave me the encouragement
to finish it and get it published.

J.B. Light

Table of Contents

1

This is a story that explains much. It will not give references to be checked because I want to present it not as a scholarly word of man but as a holy word of the Lord. However, you can check for yourself the truth of that which is stated as fact. Remember, we heard no more of Cain after God put him out of Eden; and remember, too, that science and the Bible both agree that Eden, the place of man's creation was in Africa. From the north of Africa to its southern tip, man was and is of darker hues.

So, when Cain left, he went to northern places not in Africa and eventually to the northern-most parts where very little sun could maintain his melanin. You know this put a scare into Cain for all the people he had known had melanin activated in their skin and his began to fade. It probably was the very mark that God had put on him to protect him. The loss of melanin would make him like the demonic ones who had been kicked out of heaven so they would not kill him.

Out of Africa, melanin is no longer activated to the same degree. Can you even imagine Cain's horror at his loss of the melanin that he had always had and always seen? When he looked upon Eve's face, he saw activated melanin. When he looked upon Adam's face, he saw the same, too. Upon Abel's face, he had always seen that same activation of melanin. As he happened upon the first lake to get a drink of water, he could already see the change in the content of his melanin just as he had displayed the change in the content of his character. His jealousy (always a function of the devil) drove him to kill his brother. Even though he had presented a gift before God that he thought would be worthy, it was not pleasing to God.

Remember we know of nothing that Abel had done to Cain, so his jealousy was of his own making. We always think we understand the one who created us, but our minds and hearts are too limited to ever understand the enormity of the One who created us in His image. We think that because we are created in His image that we can know Him like He knows us, but we must first recognize how vastly different He is from us and we are from Him. I am not a small fraction of who He is, so understanding and knowing Him is out of the question. But seek Him daily, I must! And truly, we must!

Getting back to Cain now. Remember he was already under the influence of the devil with the jealousy that led to the killing of his brother. When he looked upon that lake to get water and saw that his melanin was deactivated, he became even more angry at God. His skin began to get lighter and lighter as he moved out of Africa into colder climates where the sun is not an ever-present friend and enemy. God created our skin to receive the sun and change from the light look of a baby to the dark skin of man and woman as the activation of the melanin takes place. Most black babies come out initially looking white and they look at the ear to see the melanin that lets them know the complexion that is forthcoming. As Cain lost his melanin over the course of time, the anger that he felt caused him to do more and more evil.

Now, God had commanded man to care for the earth; but those like Cain thought, *why should I care for it when I can command it and make it do my will?*. Because we think we know God, we are presumptive enough to believe that He approves of whatever we do. Having forgotten the evil that we've inherited from Cain, we justify all kinds of evil now.

It saddens me when people in European countries and in the USA call for making their countries "white" again. Every American is an African American no matter how much of their hue has been lost. Many people started using Ancestry, the supposed DNA company, to find out that they are European, which they equate to white. When the tests began coming back with percentages from Africa, the company then began offering to omit those percentages by checking a box at the bottom of the application. It made people feel better about themselves, but it still didn't change the fact of the percentages that gave proof that they had African blood.

We forget that just like America, England had slavery, and like America, Englishmen raped the black enslaved and produced biracial children who were lighter and later were raped to produce more children who had lost their darker hues that came out of Africa. When the enslaved of England declared an end to the enslavement, those light enough to pass for white did so, just as they did in the good old USA.

In 2021 after Trump's newest loss, that of the presidency, hueloss people began calling more and more for a return to a "white" country. How they couldn't believe he lost legitimately is beyond me, because just as Aretha Franklin was a stone singer, Trump has been a stone loser all his life. He has been fraudulent all his life too and my heart cries out for those who support his lies that an election was stolen.

I know God is on the throne and no gold replica of Trump will ever replace Him. God will eventually curse those preachers who are calling on their people to kill blacks and/or democrats in support of Trump. Remember, satan is he who has to use lies and deceit, not our Lord. I pray for those people who have gotten caught up in the new lies of racism. You may think that my remark about everyone being African American was just my thinking/talking in terms of those who may have a portion of African ancestry; but truth be told, all men have African ancestry, though some may have left the continent (or their forebears of course) with Cain from so long ago that even traces of that ancestry will no longer show up.

Understanding that our modern ancestry tests, for the most part, only track more recent generations because they lack the specificity needed to decisively trace all the way back to Africa. Since God created man in Africa, on which the Bible and science both agree, then no matter how long our forebears have been out of Africa to have created the loss of hue, Africa is still our ancestral home for all man.

You would think that those who call themselves Christians would know this and accept this. Just because hueloss has caused some people to lighten greatly, if you stay in the sun your tan will come. It's almost hilarious to think of how people buy expensive tanning beds to get a darker hue/ yet have the audacity to hate those with a natural darker hue.

Could it be that the real hatred is because they know that melanin is strength? When you keep a person down, so you don't have to compete, it's never strength on your part. If you truly believe that darker hues are lesser, then there would be no need to keep them down. You would want to help them by giving them even more chances. Another thing that is hilarious is hueloss people saying that darker hued people are lazy. Think for a moment... *Did hued or hueloss people make America wealthy by their sweat and work?* If you're honest you would have to say no. You sat on the veranda while the darker hued people did the work. Many didn't even nurse their own babies. Enslaved women had to reserve one breast for the hueloss woman's child as though the breast that the enslaved woman used for her child wasn't good enough for the other. Ridiculous, isn't it? But remember America isn't racist! If we examine our history though, we would have to admit that truly it is. Just like the rest of the world.

But remember, there is a way out of this craziness. Please remember that it was not all of those who had lost much of their hue that operated in the slavery market. Those with a little money were able to become wealthy by trading in the slave market. Those who were poor were free but lacked many of the necessities of life as the enslaved did. It wasn't initially the poor whites who hated the enslaved. They were taught to hate them by the enriched class, so that they would then support their evil. A hueloss man could only vote if he owned property. The ruling class had to keep them from blaming the wealthy for their lack, so turning them against the enslaved was designed to keep the ruling class protected from the masses.

Man, who claims to love God/Christ and yet hates others, lies to people and more disastrously lies to himself. Even today the Southern Baptists that were founded on racism seem unable to part ways with it. They may now call themselves Evangelicals—"Super Christians", yet they change the Bible to use race for people when race was used for a contest only. The Bible doesn't mention races of people because there is only one race--The human race-- that our God created. He made not man and woman, but instead made 'man'--male and female-- He made us.

3

There was no curse put on Africans, because we were all Africans then. The poor hueloss man has been taught to hate the hued, just so the rich can enslave their minds as they had enslaved the hued one's bodies. They say they are for the poor hueloss ones, but you need to wise up and see the truth. If you keep your focus on keeping the hued population down, you fail to see what they are doing to you.

Remember, if you keep your foot on someone, they can't move, **but neither can you**. Research shows how much we have lost financially by keeping hued people down. Remember Tulsa--those hued people had 7--count again--7 private planes. That one community had so much wealth that the hueloss wealthy kept pointing to them as the reason that the hueloss ones were in poverty. Of course, as in so many cases that was a lie. It is so sad that one realizing their inability to compete resorts to demonizing others and pointing out differences to bring great contention, mistrust, and negativity between and among groups of people. America isn't racist, yet they taught natives and children of color to root for the white (hueloss) man to always beat/dominate the native Americans. When you're so embarrassed about your history that you keep lying about the truth of your history, you will never grow. Our Lord is calling us to repentance. Wake up and hear His voice.

Hueloss Americans keep saying they built this country and made it rich, yet history tells a very different story. Native Americans, African Americans, Chinese Americans, all gave the greatest contributions to the wealth of this nation. And it has been added to by many others from around the world. If our hueloss ones would accept the truth, teach the truth and repent of that truth our nation would and could be far, far better than it is. As long as deep divisions remain, the benefit is only to the wealthy who never say that they have enough, and we will continue to struggle over the same things.

How is it that we tolerate some people being trillionaires, yet are paying a small amount in taxes while we have veterans living on the street? They believe that they are prudent and shrewd; so to take the focus off themselves, they lead the march in the belief that their rights as hueloss ones are being taken from them and they often do it through their churches. How can hueloss men claim that they are being discriminated against just because others are also showing a lesser level of poverty?

Claiming that the government has given those who are hued all the breaks is absurd. The Southern Baptists supported slavery and had the audacity to use the Bible to support the evil belief that it was God ordained. God told Adam that **he would labor to support himself,** not to enslave another to do it for him. Yet preachers supported the landowners, rather than leading them to repentance. It is amazing that the very lies that can be shown to be racist or sexist are maintained and increased, rather than leading us to a more perfect union.

I thought in my many years that I had seen all that could possibly be seen when it comes to people, but with the advent of Trump and the QAnon faction that believes not only him but also believe the conspiracy theories that keep popping up and changing, I've seen it all now. Unbelievable how people who call themselves Christians can't tell the devil from God! Unfortunately, someone like Trump, who learned the trade tactics of a grifter, learned the tactics far too well. God has asked that we tell the truth, yet Trump has them believing lies. All throughout the election cycle of 2020, his polling results showed him losing, yet he continually told his crowds that he would win by wide margins.

Unfortunately, Fox news is equally to blame. When a people use only one source of information they are more easily duped. Fox news decided to support Trump and his minions in whatever lie they told.

Yet, God will not hold those who claim his name guiltless because even with all the changes that people have made to the Bible to support man's way of thinking, His Word still stands as our truth.

4

Did you ever wonder why if the Bible is really believed to be God's word to us, why they keep changing it? Look at all the times they changed servant in the King James to slave in newer versions. I believe that it may have been done to support slavery in England, other parts of Europe, and throughout the United States. In 2021 I still hear the hueloss say slavery was OK because it was in the Bible. Any true child of God is able to hear the Holy Spirit speak and lets us know right from wrong. When the good of today is spoken of as evil then we should know that we've fallen far away from the will of God.

On July 4, 2021, Vanessa Williams sang Lift Every Voice during the PBS celebration. I read many slanderous insults toward her and PBS in calling it divisive. They called the recognition of Juneteenth divisive also. Yet so few call many acts by white supremacists divisive. Man may call evil that which is good, but God still calls it evil. Man will pay mightily in the afterlife in which they say they believe. If they really believed in the afterlife, their behavior on earth would be far different.

I pray for my racist and sexist, delusional brothers and sisters who have made money their God. They view Trump as a successful businessman, yet most of his businesses have failed. He does show himself to be a great grifter, however. That was their excuse they said for supporting him, yet our Lord reads hearts and minds and knows the truth. It has been shown that racism was the driving force for his support by those who call themselves Christians. Money has been the God of America that far too many have accepted as worthy. Ask yourself if God will find you worthy at your demise. Hopefully, you recognize at some point that you should have shame and go before the Lord with a contrite heart and desire a repentant spirit.

My heart aches for brothers and sisters who go to church and are taught to hate rather than to love. Beware of the web of lies that you've woven, for they will return to strangle you. God is still on the throne. He alone has the throne and shares it with no one. The golden image of Trump was viewed by him and his followers as a very positive thing, but the God who rules the whole universe thought of it as a mockery. Many of their preachers even supported it as they support Trump because they, too, have made money and power their god. Out of the heart of a man is revealed his soul.

I'd rather be black as tar on the outside rather than black on the inside. Black on the inside makes you devoid of light. Without the light of the Lord, you will continue to believe that right is wrong and wrong is right. You see no evil in demanding that a young child give birth to a baby implanted by incest or rape. Yet you set up those very children that you demand be born in a world of slow death. Who are you to reign supreme over someone else's body? The jails are full of those children that you forced to be here, yet you've refused to take care of once they were here. Is it more just to die a quick death before full term or a slow death in a reckless society that hates you once you are born?

How do we convince those who are afraid of the truth to embrace truth so that they can be free? Repentance is what has to happen in America, but unless truth is known, repentance won't come. Any attempts to embrace the truth is now called reverse racism. They even tell the hued to blame their forefathers, who sold them into slavery, to keep themselves from any responsibility. Like Adam and Eve, shifting the blame for what is done never works. It's sad when our guilt causes us to shift the blame, rather than embracing it in repentance, for then the matter for which we need to repent never goes away.

I pray that someone somewhere will begin to call for the repentance of slavery and recognize how America was built on the backs of enslaved people, on land stolen from natives. How much is even being produced today by those still enslaved because prison still enforces legal slavery? We must recognize every group that made America strong and repent of the evil that makes America weak. Think about this: if you stand on my neck, true, I can't move **but neither can you.**

5

You see by now that you simply keep going backwards, rather than forward. We must learn to repent the truth of our evil and begin to work together for the good of all, as it is called for in the word of God. We must act as true Christians for a change by denouncing any preacher using the Bible to divide, rather than bringing us together.

Lord, it looks as though Republicans are really ready to make every effort to overcome our democracy. I've heard several congressmen and senators of that party stating that we aren't supposed to have a democracy, but a republic. They seem to be trying to bypass a republic and head straight to a dictatorship, with Trump as the head. He does not care if he has to destroy this whole system of government, in order to save himself. He is still lying in an effort to divide. Fox News and others are aiding and abetting in that evil process.

Only this morning, I heard that the Senate will not pass the budget for the Capitol police. Are they planning another insurrection and don't want the CP to have the capacity to stop it this time? What have we become under Trump? Generals willing to lie and work with our enemies to get Trump elected. Trump was able to pardon those who had been found guilty in those endeavors and in lying to Mueller during the Russian investigation, but God gave Biden the election to stop his evil.

Don't the Republicans recognize that even now Putin is doing all he can to destabilize America in order to destabilize the world? Lord, we need you to take those out who want to destabilize the world for self-gain! We must realize that, based on our history in the USA, there is reason to fear the rising tide of hatred. One governor just signed a bill to teach Asian American history, yet another (more than one actually) outlawed the teaching of African American history from 1619, when the first slaves came to what was known as the New World.

Even the story of Ruby Bridges is now being banned from schools because they say that it presents "white" in a bad light. The truth is still the truth. We made the light in which we are seen; and rather than hiding from it, let's admit the truth and get into a spirit of repentance and away from the spirit of rejection of truth. When you push it out so it cannot to be taught, it inflicts greater damage, because the evil is hidden and never repented.

It saddens my heart that people can say they love the Lord and have no idea of what that love requires. We can't love Him directly, so He has made it clear how we are to demonstrate our love for Him. We must love Him by loving others. How does one study or even just read the Bible and miss this? Jesus' words in red-inked Bibles tell us the truth. Yet, man has made so many changes to the Bible that fulfills their fantasy of lies.

And, once again, God created only one race, the human race of mankind, not races. He didn't create man and woman. He created man, male and female. He created them. Adam gave Eve the woman version. *WO* at first may have been *Wow* because of his excitement in seeing that naked female. It may have turned to *Woo* at the realization that he needed to woo her to get what he wanted from her. In time it turned to "Woe" when he threw her under the bus because his behavior provoked God's wrath.

Too many have used God's word to keep a straight-jacket on females, but everything that applies to a man applies to her as well. When you don't truly know God, you can't know yourself or those with whom you are supposed to be in communion. Oh, the shame of it that has caused so much horror. Horror in committing outrageous acts from boyish fear from those who declare themselves men, horror in hiding the acts so that no one will know and see the truth of who you are, and horror that you have such little balls that you can't even admit truth to yourself and repent of it. Horror that you maintain lies of superiority because you need to see yourself in some deceptive way. My heart bleeds for you and pleads with you. There is truth be known, and for once repent rather than hide.

Lord, I send up prayers for my brothers and sisters who somehow believe that they are in Christ, yet still don't know You. Reveal to them Lord an accurate rendering of Your word and will so that they are not following a preacher, pastor, prophet with evil intent, but they are actually following You. Have them read the words of Jesus so that their claim of being His followers can become their truth. Lord, heal all of our hearts from fear of what is going on in our country at present. Some say Latinos voted for Trump because of their fear of communism, yet they fail to realize that it only exists under a dictatorship, which Trump appeared to try to bring about. Though he is no longer in office, he is still trying to bring it about. Please help America wake up.

Lord, help us repent of slavery, repent of racism, and take You as our Lord rather than money and power. That's what communists do. Only the ones at the top get the wealth. I was sending money to Jews in Russia who were starving. If communism worked under Putin, I would never have had to do that. Please Lord, wake America up to truth and repentance. God has promised that anything I ask in His name shall be done. Lord, again I come before you, asking for healing for this country.

Trump continues to use Putin's playbook to divide us along racial lines. He presents blacks as hating the country and lumps them in with Democrats to make people believe that blacks are the Democratic Party and want to replace the hueloss of America. How it is that they can't see truth is beyond me. Lord, I ask that You give those who claim You, true spiritual discernment so that they can subtract themselves from subversive mindsets and behaviors.

Fear can be deadly. We saw the evidence of it on Jan. 6th. Having someone cause you to believe certain things can provoke a level of fear of the unknown. Fox media is as much to blame as Trump himself, as they have supported his lies though they well know the truth. The people themselves are responsible also, because they are receiving what they want to believe. Sponsors of the media are also to blame, claiming a lack of knowledge of the propaganda put forth by those they support. Some of Americas wealthiest are supporting Putin against Ukraine right now.

Both of our cars are from a company that gave financial support to seditionists. We were looking to purchase another one, but since they gave financial backing to the seditious members of Congress, no longer can we purchase their vehicles. Their cars do tend to last almost forever, but our values can't be bought by that factor over others that are deemed more important. These companies must not realize that they are adding to America's loss of its democracy, or do they? The ethos of companies can no longer be the bottom line of economics, but the values that they stand for.

Branson just took a group of people to outer space for a joyride to start a new venture of joyrides to space at a price of 250k per person. Yet we have many veterans and others living in their cars, on the streets, or in shelters provided by others. The dollar seems to be more and more the God of America. Will that be the sword that we end up dying by, too? I pray that we won't allow that to happen. Not just in my lifetime, but ever!

My heart breaks on the level of ignorance of the hueloss who are believing so many lies. How can they not know that their origins go back to Africa, just as all men? The Bible and science both agree. Both of these constructs were given by God to man through inspiration. How can we disavow one and pit one against the other? I thank You, God, and await to see Your mighty hand in this situation that is trying to destroy democracy.

America with all its faults had to be God's idea because of what He had racist men write in our Preamble and Constitution. Some of them denounced slavery, but many of them were enslavers. Though most claimed to be Christians they raped enslaved girls and had babies by them that they didn't free in their lifetime and some even after that. Hueloss people even put their names on achievements of slaves because the enslaved were disenfranchised. I hear hueloss people say and write that African Americans shouldn't have a problem with American enslavers because it was the forebears in Africa that sometimes captured the enslaved and sold them first. What rationalization!

Invisible to self-knowledge shows that some hueloss follow satan rather than Christ Jesus, for a true relationship with Christ shows us the truth of ourselves. My heart wrenches for my hueloss brothers and sisters who mistakenly follow the darkness of satan rather than the light of Christ, yet verbally claim that they follow Christ. They truly need to read the red-letter words of Jesus Christ in the New Testament to know how to be a Christian. Lord, let the preachers, pastors, and prophets return to this in their churches this coming Sunday. This I pray and expect to see reports of the same. Thank you, Lord!

Did Cain believe, even though he was in the very presence of God? I think not. Let's take a deep dive into what the spirit of Cain was, still is and how it presented itself then and presents itself even now. Cain was born in Africa, just as Adam and Eve had been created there. The Bible and science both agree that man had its beginning in Africa, so all people started off as what is called black in the very jungles of Africa. If people would just understand this small truth, then there would be fewer problems in the world for we are all related, by God's determination. Can you imagine what He thinks about us as we call blacks evil and whites the devil? I know if my heart can be broken by such, His must be too, as our Creator.

As we look back on who you would call black Cain and explore the spirit man of this created being, we see that God has allowed the spirit of selfishness, which leads to evil doings. God never cursed Cain's offering but nonetheless he became angry because God applauded Abel's offering. Instead of Cain trying to figure out how to do better in glorifying God, he instead chose to murder his brother.

God, as creator, knows our hearts, minds, and spirits and knows the essence of 'usness' through these. He knew the heart, mind, and spirit of Cain's offering. Mindless to the big Who of God, he gave an offering that he thought little of. We have tried to explain God's reaction to Abel and Cain by looking at the gifts themselves, but we really can't adequately figure it out.

Throughout the Bible, the food first thought of as good are vegetables. That's what Cain gave. To kill an innocent animal was often thought of as a negative. Well, that's what Abel gave and his giving, not what he gave, was acceptable to God. This applies to us today, sidebar, the phony fight for life in the womb; yet creating these conditions that cause suffering by children so they may have a negative relationship in society at the hands of educators, police, and the criminal justice system is simply a farce created to pretend caring about others. Which is more merciful in God's sight? Is it the babe in the womb or the child /person after birth? How we treat the least of these persons is what our Lord judges. Selah. (Think about it)

Right now, my heart is bleeding for the youth and children throughout the U S who are sick and dying because Fox News and Republican personalities are pushing COVID as nothing. They pushed vaccinations under Trump, but the messaging changed because Biden came in so robustly to address the need, and the numbers of positive cases went far down. If people hate so much that they are willing to let you and your children suffer so that Biden's Covid death numbers increase and won't make Trump look so bad, how do you even support such persons?

It's ironic that the Republicans are calling themselves "for the average people"; yet their support goes against average Americans and instead to corporations, the wealthy, and businesses that pour into their coffers all in the effort to keep the poor supporting the country; and the rich are just getting richer. To deprive the IRS of finances to audit the wealthy is unjust. Some Republicans are now talking about doing away with Social Security. I have a bridge that I can sell you if you're willing to believe their bag of lies!

Back to the spirit of Cain. I haven't read Josephus who has given more information about Cain, but Holy Spirit speaks truth to those who are true believers. Evil was the spirit of Cain from the beginning. From evil comes competition on an emotional level, comparisons, spite, selfishness and all the other ills of a society. When people have been sorely mistreated one may be able to understand why they engage in evil and yet so much evil comes from those hueloss who claim to have been brought up in wealth or at least have had the benefits of a stable middle-class home life.

That Cain spirit is seen in so many of our politicians who purport to be for the average man. Refusal to issue or keep mask mandates, which exposes more and more people to COVID doesn't seem to speak to that claimed truth. How then does the spirit of Cain, that evil seed keep progressing? Does genetics play a role? We can never know but we see it more and more. Look at Tucker Carlson, who nightly fans the flames of racial hatred by asserting that African Americans with hue want to replace the hueloss. If we just tell the hueloss the truth that they are Africans also, maybe they could ignore Tucker's clueless rhetoric and choose to believe that which is less divisive.

God gave all man melanin. Melanin serves as strength, but activated melatonin has been demonized by the religious community for far too long to easily change the mind of those with the Cain spirit. When Cain was put out, he probably went north. As he traveled north, less melanin activation took place so his hue would become lighter, and each successive generation would become lighter and lighter. It's funny how people take pride in their loss of melanin and it's heartbreaking how they have and do regularly demonize those who show their melanin. Selah (remember to just think about it)

Imagine that Cain, as he moved to northern climates, began noticing that he was losing his hue. What was he losing, you say? The activation of his melanin was decreasing in each successive generation more and more. He had to recognize it as a loss rather than as something to make him superior. Thick curls of hair that provided protection from the sun to the scalp was now long and stringy. His nose decreased in size to better block out the cold air. Without the intensity of the sun, now lighter hair, skin and eyes – all indicating a loss of melanin activation.

When Cain recognizes that he's lost something, what does that Cain spirit do? Claim it as a gain, a win and just what God intended for man. And he justifies his loss as something superior and his loss as a negative to be attributed to those who have little or no loss of hue. Many people believe that those we call "white" today don't realize that they too came from Africa. They have been students of the Bible far longer than I have yet don't recognize truth.

We claim the Bible to be God's word to us, yet continuously use it for evil. Justification of slavery of African Americans was never approved of in His word, just in the spirit, because of your true God - money. Look at Tom Jefferson, speaking against slavery, yet keeping far more slaves than the average because they brought him so much money and he even had many children by his wife's half-sister who were all enslaved.

The wealth of the United States was indeed created by enslaved Africans and yet those slaves were denied in every avenue to have any right to what they worked for. When you investigate yourself, seek and see truth, speak truth, and may you break the back of that evil that has so easily beset you. Please don't continue to be a man of emptiness. Many of the fathers of the U. S were men of emptiness because they could rape a young, enslaved girl making her an object of hatred by his wife and making her children caretakers of his children by his wife of marriage.

That Cain spirit let's man justify anything! The most vile thing disguised as good, and a malevolence disguised as benevolence so that people can't come out against it. We must start seeing truth, speaking truth, and living truth if we are to have any hope of a life everlasting. For just as Cain couldn't fool God, neither can we. He sees that money and power are the gods of America though we claim otherwise.

I pray that the heart of man receives a direct message from God and embraces it, so that it brings him to his knees and also to the very heart of God. Then, maybe we can hear from God rather than keep the messages of satan alive. Satan only thrives in the spirit of Cain. The Cain spirit of hueloss people always looks for the advantage. If they don't have it naturally, they will try to create circumstances by which they can or at least pretend to obtain it.

For the hundreds of years of slavery in the United States, the enslaved were not allowed to learn to read. Funny how that led the Cain spirit to believe that they were of superior intellect because the enslaved were subjugated to their rule of authority and not allowed to learn to read. Hueloss people have maintained the system of vast inequality over hundreds of years and yet when many of those coming from formerly enslaved families and being relegated to inferior communities, including schools, didn't display the refinement of culture that they didn't even know, the enslavers could then say that they were of lower intelligence.

Intelligence scales were just another part of the lie to try to bring truth to racist ideology. So many of our belief patterns were artificially constructed to try to show an advantage for the hueloss because of their true feelings of inadequacy. They put their names on inventions by the enslaved and wanted no one to question the legitimacy that they claimed. A whole construct of inequality had to be constructed and maintained for the lies to be believed. Reinforced over hundreds of years, the lies have stuck and the hueloss are able to believe the lie of superiority as a result. God shares his throne with no one. Some may have forgotten this, but He never forgets. The day of reckoning is nigh. (Selah).

It's appalling that Trump is now being compared to Hitler, since his divisive ideology and support for supremacy of the hueloss spoke volumes from the very beginning. Hitler was only loyal to Hitler, never to those he used for his own purposes. When people don't read, study, and gain knowledge they repeat the same errors of history, time and time again.

What a price we will pay for using a pretext of Christ in our lives, when satan has full reign. What will Terrell and Candace do when the "white" supremacists take over the United States that you have helped them to secure? Do you really think they will love you with your dark-hued skin because you supported them in their evil? Even minorities who don't have darkened melanin of skin will be treated no better than those with the darkest hues. My heart bleeds for my brethren who believed that if they too hate darker melanin people that they will be considered one of the majority rather than a minority.

America has done a pervasive job of increasing hatred against darker melanin, but also against every other minority. Can you imagine dark melanin little boys rooting for the Indian in the western shows? No, all little boys were so impacted by racism that they rooted for the hueloss to win wars against the natives. I wonder did our little native boys cheer on in the same way. The new movie "In the Heights" is catching grief now because they used a cast of vastly lighter hued Hispanics. This too is a result of the caste system in America.

The closer you are to the melanin of majority America, the higher esteemed you are. It's sad to see the anger of our darker hued brothers and sisters turned against themselves. When they riot and tear down their own neighborhoods, or kill and maim within those same neighborhoods, it tells the story of how the minds have been so damaged that they destroy themselves rather than the antagonists who get them to do just that. The only ones of their community that they should fight against are the drug dealers and those who furnish the money for those drugs to destroy the communities within as they continue to devise means to destroy within and without.

They are finally trying to change Amendment 13. The Cain spirit has set up private prisons to function as corporations for some rich to be made richer off the backs of hued brothers and sisters often spending time in this legal slavery system, having done nothing more than having a deodorizer hanging from a car mirror. Only a Cain spirit could even decide and devise such a thing.

Cain spirit people will claim God because they recognize His power but it's always just a ruse to get other people to love and respect them while they love and respect no one. They know that God knows the evil in their hearts and minds, but of that they care not. As long as they can get some people following them, they continue to walk in deeper and wider evil until they die. Death brings not an end to it, for by then, they have indoctrinated so many more in the vast array of evil who carry it forth. They are good at manipulation because they study people to see what gets the desired reactions and they respond just like the experienced fisherman. He never pulls them in fast but slowly, so they never know that they are being lured in until it's too late.

So many of the Cains of today are racists who see too many rights being granted to others. Even though others gaining rights doesn't take away any of theirs, the very idea of others having the very same rights and putting them on equal footing is perceived as a diminishment of their rights. If we all have the same rights, how then am I able to maintain my claim of superiority. The minds of the Cains are bad, but the mind of a hueloss Cain is even worse.

Having been birthed in a country where loss of hue makes one superior rankles less heavily. Our mindset birthed and reinforced by the government policies gave and continues to give rise to fear of

37

change. In the new movement for human and civil rights, we see youth fight for equal justice and older one's fight for QAnon. The older ones use it to maintain their spiritual superiority (so they think) to justify any amount of evil that they choose to exert over people and or policies that came against their false beliefs. For them we must pray for their heart, mind, and spiritual changes or that they will simply die out. Unfortunately, they don't die out until they have infected others, even if on a diminished level. With the same evil, McCarthy named several congressmen who voted not to certify the legal votes of Joe Biden's presidency to the investigative board for January 6th.

10

It's truly sad how they keep talking about BLM as needing investigation as though it compares to white supremacy. They are trying mightily to get BLM labeled as a hate group. Paid antagonists and self-called "white supremacists" were the ones who caused so much of the damage during BLM protests. Yet they prefer jailing BLM for marching for justice rather than giving apt punishment for those who made the insurrection against our very country. Cries for equality being compared to demands to put a dictator in power don't seem to equate, much less to be about equity. Equity now seems to be a non-starter. The new Texas law that the Ku Klux Klan cannot be taught as an evil group gives one pause to wonder what exactly is in the minds of people. The Bible says evil will be called good and good called evil and that appears to be what is now happening more and more.

I would like to say that the end time has arrived, but it's always been so. Many people before and now have been doing it since the writing of the Bible. Christians so often have followed a set of rules that may have no identity with Christ, yet it's what they followed to be esteemed by self and others as the model for a Christian. How easily we delude ourselves under the cover of that false Christian banner. Falwell Sr. was said to be a racist; but he was well respected as a Christian by man, but never by Christ. Though they claim an afterlife, we can tell that they truly don't believe in Christ by their very actions here on earth while they are alive. All I can say here is "God, please awaken them to truth". (Selah)

Why does America not want the truth of America to become known? It probably isn't because of its racist past. Just yesterday, I read about a man using his racism against a disabled black teen and he declared that "white" people had made this country rich. He believes that "white" people built this country. You see what not knowing truth is able to do! You hold the present with lies of the past and hopes and expectations of holding the future. This leaves God out of the picture, rather than as the final arbiter of all things. There was no mistake that the Lord allowed Africans to be sold into slavery in Europe and the Americas. A democratic society of equality was what He probably had in mind that fostered full acknowledgment of Him by our actions, not just empty words. Though Jefferson was a founding father and a very important figure in our history, he was a slaveholder because of his admitted greed, and he knew the evils of slavery and wrote about it. Having been one of the leaders to draft *The Declaration of Independence* and wrote that God ordained "*all men are created equal and are endowed by their Creator with certain inalienable rights*" yet not giving these rights to those who were not hueloss. Changes in the racist behavior have continuously gone back to this time and time again.

In the 2020's we see man returning to his racist past in America, yet the fight for true justice and true equality lives on in the hearts and minds of many of the citizens. Fox News will be heavily punished due to its push for division along hue lines in this country. They know viewership could be increased with their support of the evils of Trump and Trumpism. They chose the evils of money over democracy and over the rights of all people.

The true Cain spirit for the Trumps came to America with the grandfather who ran whore houses and sold liquor. Always ones to capitalize off others, the Cain spirit has fostered true evil in that family. They don't even recognize the truth of themselves because of their depth of evil. Lying is thought of as normal, rather than deviant. Playing people for suckers is considered a sporting ambition, never considering God and His authority. Preachers were conned because they wanted to be conned due to the evil in their own hearts. They too forgot that God shares his throne with no one!

41

God will never share His throne because it is His alone. Though three persons (personalities) in one God, He alone is God. Though my heart aches for those who are lonely and are getting caught up in the evil of Trump's and Republicans' lies of politics, I still hold them guilty for abandoning our great God for a deluded impostor who knows that he is purposefully manipulating people. I ask not for a change of heart for him and them but for a change that only God can bring. Let them see the actual evil of what they do and think. They don't have to keep the spirit of Cain. They can seek God through prayer and His word on a constant and consistent basis to realize the truth. Some realize the truth yet continue in the folly of Trump's lies for self-gain. This simply proves once again that money is their God. When we acknowledge that God doesn't share his throne, that easily includes money.

11

Most of the evils of the U.S. Have been implemented and practiced due to the hold that money has had and continues to have on its people. Money itself is never evil, but often what people are willing to do for it constitutes the evil. Let's start at the beginning, not 1776, but indeed 1619. We can fool ourselves that the U.S. birth was 1776, but it truly was 1619 because the laws began to change from indentured servants to chattel slavery. Why would the law change for birth from the position of the child tied to the father to now being tied to the mother?

Those Europeans who were raping the African indentured servants, who then became slaves for life, would now birth children of the slave masters who became slaves for life because they now followed the position of the mother, rather than the father. The laws equating a dark skin to lifelong servitude, rather than the original seven years was now enforced. Minds of greed and thoughts of wealth and power led to all of this and in our modern time the efforts to restrict voting are for the same purposes.

Critical Race Theory is but a construct to explain how the use of "race" which doesn't even exist led to an America in which laws and mindsets have been so corrupted that it led to real damage to groups of people based on skin color. Even among African Americans who maintained their hue, the lighter hues were held in higher esteem. We are all African Americans, even those who call themselves Proud Boys, Aryan Brotherhood, or any other "white" supremacist name. They are all lying to themselves. They know that the loss of their hue created a real loss therefore they had to create laws by any means to keep the hued to a lower level in society without rights or powers. Give a hued person a bone and they can make soup. No one must teach them this. All men are created equal by God, yet some men want to strip away the rights of God and give it to themselves. God will never share His throne. (Selah)

The Delta Variant is beginning to attack the unvaccinated to a degree that is causing Republican governors to plead with the people to get the vaccine. Many have been undercutting what President Biden has been doing to try to stop the virus. They have come out with mandates against quarantining, against vaccines, and even against a simple mask to protect people. Making laws and issuing decrees against things that stop the spread are being recognized as those things that kill the ones expected to vote Republican.

It is truly sad when the political ambitions of one political party are so diabolical as to cause high levels of death once again. The level of ignorance on what is called the "Right" is tragic. If they would stop speaking, that ignorance could not spread; but unfortunately they are truly too dumb to even know what they don't know. Their ignorance will eventually kill over a million Americans. My heart breaks for those of that mindset who are now awakening to the truth and asking for vaccines, while in the hospital ready for intubation. The doctors can only tell them at that point, that it's too late.

The ones calling themselves religious or even Christian on the right gave such power to an evil clown and his family that it will take over a decade to get things back to a semblance of what we were headed for. True democracy exists only with rights for all, regardless of "race" or social economic levels. I thought we were moving in that direction and could possibly achieve it in my lifetime, but here we go again! Restrictive voting laws, frivolous voting audits, and lies in abundance to make people afraid of each other. God is still on the throne and God shares his throne with no one. See what the Lord will do. (Selah)

I wonder why they allow Trump to continue the rallies of lies. Just him having them makes more and more people believe the lies that he spews forth. I am concerned about the greater divisiveness that he is stoking. One councilman even asked, "where is the house nigger", Something of that nature may have been thought, but not said, previously. Now it's as if the hueloss have returned to mindsets of the 1800s when the enslaved were freed on paper, but the hueloss maintained all power over them still.

God has mandated that America be the land of opportunity for all people. How much wickedness will we put up with because of skin tones? Ancestry.com had to put a box to check if a person didn't want to receive the African ancestry when they are predominantly European. Before that was added people were receiving reports that they were 8 -15% African which some deemed as a plot against "white supremacy" beliefs. Remember, any African blood at all made one African American. The truth would set you free if you would but seek the truth, accept the truth, and live with and by that truth.

It is much harder to hate than to love. Our Lord leads the charge in love which He made our natural, innate nature. We must choose outside of our Creator to allow satan to lead us to jealousy, fear, competition and finally hatred. Melanin will always be a strength. Why get jealous when those with it can compete at high levels in anything. Why would the slaves be kept from learning to read? It wasn't because the enslavers thought them lacking in intelligence. No laws would have been made against it if that were true.

Hued persons have no desire to replace people, but instead desire to live a life worthy of the calling of God. You look too low if you believe there could be a desire to replace you. Only a spirit of Cain could bring about this belief. It hurts me to see other hueloss people leading the lie of replacement theory to make money. Even hued ones get in on the evil for selfish gain as well, showing that the Cain spirit is not just in the hueloss, but is a choice chosen by far too many who think that money and evil influence will give them the benefits of life to which they aspire. The hued ones who bombard the airwaves with "racism" are still to be loved, yet pitied, for that soul hates itself. Only a lost soul can lose itself so completely as to sell that soul to the highest bidder. Satan will always be the highest bidder for evil, while God will have no part in it.

We must decide that money will never be our God, or we can never say "enough". We can get caught deeper and deeper into our reliance on comfort that we make choices not of God, but of satan, leaving us with no ability to understand that evil will never say enough. We must use our God-given fortitude to say no to the pull of the world way and yes to God's way. We have no excuse for getting it backwards. (Selah)

Jeremiah 22:13 "Woe To him who builds his palace by unrighteousness, his upper rooms by injustice, making his own people work for nothing". This has been used as justification to make those of darker hues live a life of servitude. People have used this scripture to justify and enslave others for successive generations because the hued people were not their own people. Even families of those enslaved often don't realize what the forefathers/mothers had to endure.

A piece of fat back from the hogs they raised was turned into a meal, showing that the enslaved learned how to do much with little. Those in the kitchen who fixed what the enslavers were to eat, were able to sneak something out. One sweet potato can make many if soaked in water and allowed to bloom. Sweet potatoes are still one of the staples of the enslaved progeny. Something that they found to be edible became a delicacy for the enslavers and sustenance for those enslaved.

Much of American cuisine can be traced back to Africa. The enslavers used "his own people" to justify enslavement of darker hued people and when some came out light enough to be white, the law was changed so that the station of the child would follow the mother who had the baby, rather than the enslavers who raped to get the baby, a point that needs repeating. Was it heartlessness that you created a human, refused to accept and care for them as your own, kept them in bondage all the days of their lives, raped them and had more babies to create your wealth? No, they had hearts and minds from the spirit of Cain.

13

Hueloss people today refuse to believe the facts of slavery because if they knew and believed the facts then they feel justified in being seen as evil. The schools under new laws are no longer allowed to teach that the KKK was and is evil. Somehow changing them from a malevolent organization to a benevolent one. Soon they will present them on a level with God. What I'm seeing in 2021 is hard to believe. Any truth about the hueloss that they view as evil must be covered up rather than exposed. Don't they realize our God sits high, looks low and has a place for each of us, based on our hearts that lead to our deeds.

Judgment awaits each of us. I pray repentance for those who call revelation of truth-evil and hiding the evil truth-good. The only way to forget and forgive the evil done is repentance. Too many declare that there is nothing for which they need to repent because they didn't enslave anyone. That is true but look at your attitude toward those of darker hues. Surely, repentance is needed. Though they continue in

51

their corruption just by other names today, such as voter suppression, prison work gangs for privately-owned prisons, public money for segregated private schools, etc. Jeremiah 22:15b-16. "Did not your father have food and drink?" He did what was right and just, so all went well with him. He defended the cause of the poor and needy and so all went well. "Is that not what it means to know me?" declares the Lord (Selah)

Jeremiah of the Old Testament proclaims the same things that Jesus does in the New Testament--Do what is right and just and defending the cause of the poor and needy is how we demonstrate that we know the Lord. Too often, we are wrong in our thinking that allows us to demand justice and privilege for ourselves, though it means being unjust to others. We justify our evil by our fleshly wants and ways. We don't even try to know the cause of the poor and needy, much less to defend it. Our wealth causes blindness to all else and anything else.

I wonder if sick minds ever have a lucid moment that could lead to reflection on life and on the Lord, which could bring about a guilty soul. From a guilty soul may then come a desire for repentance. For when God shows any of us the truth there is always reason to repent. How does the Lord look upon us when we are always looking to gain at the expense of someone else? His look is never one of favor when he sees the evil in our hearts that we think is so well hidden. Abortion, we cry, what an abomination, yet we readily put every type of drug in the communities, every kind of grift by the churches and politicians far too often and free slave labor in the prison system.

With generations of degradation and injustice of their forebears leaving them without skills, we claim we want life for them. Demanding life for them makes us feel good and then we declare that we gave them a chance just by demanding that they be born. I hate the very thought that a baby in a womb must die, but I hate even more that there are those who demand privilege over a woman's body that is not their own. How can I demand that another body bring forth that life unless I am ready to take care of the child or take care of the mother and the child?

It's presumptuous to think that anyone has the privilege of demanding what another does with their own body. Let us instead show value to those alive so that they can grow up and make responsible decisions for themselves. One observation made in life is that those who show themselves against something actually have some things in the closet that bring them shame. The worst attacks against homosexuals are done by closet homosexuals who feel negatively about their own desires and are frustrated when they see others with the same desires able to live a life of clarity (Selah)

G od's message to us in Jeremiah 23:10-14 should give us pause to examine ourselves and pray until we hear God's voice to us. We see today as in verse 11 that prophets and priests (pastors) are indeed godless as they proclaimed Trump would win the election. God spoke to me that Biden would win and that the Democrats would have all three houses. It would be called a lie, by the very ones who prophesied the opposite. They hear not from God because their hearts and minds are not in communion with Him but instead are in communion with satan.

This gave and continues to give support to Trump's lies that have divided our country. God declares that he will bring disaster on them for their evil. Verse 14 speaks of how horrible they are as he sees them. They commit adultery and live a lie, knowing that satan is the father of lies and liars. Yet they stay in lock step with satan rather than turning to God. They strengthened the hands of the evil-doers and their minions. Instead of helping them turn to God, they reinforced them in their evil deeds.

Even Nixon's administration of evil was no match for Trump's. More and more will come out in the commission investigating the January 6th insurrection. They will find Trump's minions' hands on the planning and execution of the seditious insurrection. Finances, contacts, speeches alike all point back to Trump. It is truly ironic that some of the dingbats of the Republican Party are claiming that the January 6th Commission is being held just to put some of them in jail. If they were traitors to the United States then they certainly need to be tried, charged, and jailed. Too many people are upset when a hued athlete turns their back on the U.S. flag, yet they have sympathy for the actual traitors who worked mightily to destroy our nation.

Turning one's back on the flag or taking a knee when the racist "Star-spangled Banner" is played does no harm to our nation. Remember, the song was written about blacks fighting for their freedom. Why was it even chosen to represent America, when we have so many beautiful and glorifying songs that don't show glee at one group's demise. The flag is supposed to represent free and brave, yet our country continues to enslave people of color in so very many ways. We place lethal chemicals in neighborhoods of color along with anything that is even thought of as toxic, we know it's only going in those communities.

Too often, it's years before the full negative impacts manifest themselves and it becomes too late to make a case. We think of the head injuries of football players as the only way to sustain the brain injuries that show up. I believe that environmental factors in the air can also produce the same type of brain damage, making black and brown youth more susceptible to the negative behaviors that come from the brain damage. The lack of impulse control by children from these environments can be seen as early as elementary school. The lack of intervention then brings a lifetime of grief for them and their families.

Too often, the poor who we have contrived to be poor and further contrived to keep them in poverty, must pay a high price in so many ways for our desire to serve the god of America-- Money. From its inception, money appears to be the main motivation, not justice, not freedom, not human rights, but the almighty dollar. Now laws are being passed to deny the truth of America. When you hide the truth of evil, it can only persist in the next generation. All people need to learn our history so that we at least have an opportunity to repent of that history. We have a great history of proclaiming our love of Christ yet hate the Jews from which He came. Remember please, that Christ was a Palestinian Jew. People will always be drawn to history and no amount of coverup can be made to keep the truth from the next generation's knowledge. God is not a man that He should lie, and the lies of man will never be hidden well enough to never see the light of day.

I pray, Lord, that one day we will repent of the enslavement of people based on darker hues, that we will admit that there are not races, but the one race that God created," the human race". Look in an older concordance from several years ago, you find race only used as a contest, never in reference to people. God sits on his throne alone, sitting high and looking low, and never sharing his throne with anyone. Though some serve a triune God, three persons in one is still God. Man will never be God and when he tries to raise himself to be such, it will always end in a very negative way. That's what January 6, 2021 was about. Foolish people were manipulated to believe a lie that led to traitors to America staging an insurrection on behalf of Trump who they can't see truthfully. Anyone with even a small measure of God could see the truth before he was even elected. How people who call themselves Christians could even vote for him is beyond belief. It must have been abetted by the pastors in the pulpit who lied like those who also abetted slavery.

15

Justification for all kinds of evil can come forth when God is not our center. When the world and things of the world hold sway, they have our minds and hearts, not God. I've never had a whole lot, but I've never been too poor to help someone else, even if it was the last that I had. It's not the limits on what we hold materially that limit what we give out, but who we truly believe holds us. When God is our true center, then we can share what we have without restraint; for we recognize that what we have is not ours, but the Lord's.

God has always been my provision and I pray will always be so. I never have to feel that sharing what I have, regardless of how little it may be, will somehow harm me and leave me with less. Though I give away much, my Lord has taught me that I can't beat God's giving. As much as I pour out to help others, He pours more in because He knows I won't hoard what He gives. By the same token, there are times when I have given when I should not have given, and He has made that gift an albatross around my neck.

A good thing to us may serve to be a really bad thing to God because it may cause others to rely on us rather than on God. It places us on the throne with God in the eyes of people. Woe to us when we give without consulting God because the good can be evil in His sight. Remember every good thing is not a God thing and we must be careful to consult Him, even in trying to do good. (Selah)

Tozer, some time ago, lamented that Christianity was no longer about Christ. 2021 has shown just how true that is; for they call themselves Christians and yet use the very word of God to support their evil towards a standard other than His own. Calling oneself a Christian will never make one so. Following the call of Christ on our lives to love keeps us in the footprints that He left for us to follow. Christianity is not a call against things but to be for what Christ stood for. I frequently ask people to get a Bible with Christ's words in red, which helps people know what following Him requires, based upon what He says.

Being against things will never make one right with Christ, but being for love, helping, kindness, and justice helps us in our true walk with the Lord. We are to be the examples of love that He has sent forth in a dark world to bring light. If we only bring darkness, then we should realize that we are acting under the authority of satan, the father of darkness and lies. Maybe that's why some of today's Christians can so readily lie to themselves that they belong to Christ, when they eagerly work for the devil. You can't belong to Christ and work for the devil. You can however fool yourself to make yourself believe such, but it is only through following satan that you can do so.

It's sad that the so-called purveyors of truth don't want the truth of America to be taught in the schools because they don't want the hueloss to feel guilt. We should all feel guilty about our justification of using human souls to build our wealth, then claiming that we ourselves did it. The truth of the matter is so much has been stolen from others, yet they were given no credit. Some are amazed when African Americans show themselves as bright and articulate as Ivanka Trump was with some of them who reportedly were on the show with her dad.

The lack of exposure to real people of color keeps so many from knowing the brilliance that exists in their minds and bodies. False evidence appearing real is what has torn America apart and is tearing us apart today. Fear is a very dangerous thing. We must realize that God has never given us a spirit of fear but of love, power, and a sound mind. Remember we have to use that power of a sound mind so that we don't become duped by evil. Power comes even before love for we must see our power against the enemy's stain of racism, since there is only one race.

16

S exism, classism, and all the other isms that divide, rather than
bring us together, must be cast aside. We must use that power to
educate the masses in truth because of our love for God who loves us
so. We are all called to be ambassadors of love. Remember love is
always stronger than hate and that's because the father of love is God
and the father of hate and lies is satan, who wants to be a god, but
never shall be. Though we see his evil activity on a grand scale today
with people believing in QAnon and the lie that Trump really won the
election. Some even believe that because they are the hueloss they
won't get COVID and more foolishness that can't be even
remembered. Satan is still the loser and our God is still the winner
because of the very power of love. (Selah)

Right now, far too many Republicans believe that their
supporters are so dumb, stupid, and malleable that they are now saying
that it was not Trump supporters who planned and created the
insurrection; though one could see clearly from the rally before with

Trump that he told them to go and stop the steal. He also told them to fight and fight hard or they would no longer have a country. Most Americans would not desire to be traitors unless they are convinced that the country is a traitor to them. Trump, as the con man that he is, has convinced many that this has happened. They are preparing for a civil war that they will lose once again. They realize not that supporting such an activity is also considered to be a traitorous act. Even though none have been charged as traitors yet, time will bring it about. Because they believe a lie of satan and his minions, they will reap the negative consequences of their belief. Though the Republicans have sworn to uphold the constitution, they instead are upholding Trump and his lies. Rudy Giuliani says he is happy to go to jail yet offers the caveat that he has done nothing for which he should go to jail for. It's remarkably sad to see how so many capitulated to a liar and lies.

Satan has done a mighty work in America, but he will once again lose. This is God's country, and He desires it to be one of heterogeneity with hued and hueloss people. Loving and respecting each other and working together to make it a place that our Lord can and will bless is what our Lord is doing and will do even more. Black Lives Matter was never intended to say that other lives don't matter. The hueloss immediately came back with All Lives Matter and Blue Lives Matter to counter the message. In other words, they were once again saying the black lives don't matter and they could use the others to bring anger, hatred and bitterness against Black Lives Matter. They hired people to pretend to be part of the movement to burn, tear down, and do many of the things seen on TV to showcase it as a Marxist movement to subvert democracy.

Many of the crimes committed during the marches were committed by white supremacist believers who wanted BLM viewed negatively. After exposing several of these they stopped exposing more as they saw a pattern and would have to report the truth. They hired poor dumb black boys who brought some destruction too because if they could pass a black face with even one action, they then could blame the entire movement. Support for BLM fell heavily because of this. It would have been so easy to change the messaging from BLM to BLM Too. This way no one could say that other lives didn't matter, but black lives matter also because they had not mattered before.

Look at the situation of Simone Biles dropping out of the Olympics of summer of 2021. Instead of grace, the right winger Republicans tarred and feathered her for her behavior. She is the best gymnast in the world, yet because she didn't let her body rule her mind, they got angry. The language used against that young lady was hurtful, but also racist. Too often black bodies are appreciated but the person of the black body is denied any resemblance of respect.

Football players were being denied disability awards because they claimed that their IQ's were lower (assumed not assured). They had to lose a greater amount of cognition to get awards for the head trauma. It's sad that an artificial instrument purposed for discrimination and used to discriminate hold such a sway over the American psyche. Intelligence is a variety of things that can't be measured by paper and pencil, yet we have allowed the lie of intelligence or lack thereof to take far too greater hold in our country. The value of a man is not the minutiae that he holds in his head but the love he holds in his heart. (Selah)

The Bible gives us warning after warning about how to treat others. Today's "Christians" seem not to have knowledge of this. Even pastors are telling their flocks to physically attack those who have a different view of justice, love, life, and liberty. Carrying the Confederate flag of sedition as traitors of the United States, they also carried what they claimed to be the Christian flag. Their actions made a mockery of the Christian flag because their ideas only included the ideas of slavery rather than the ideals of Jesus Christ. How they reconcile the two is anyone's guess, but the pastors of Evangelical churches have had a commanding hand in it. The lack of love showcases one's true relationship with Christ Jesus. Even if a mind demented enough can sow hate toward a group of people because of their hue and believe they are right with God, it does in no way make them the Christians that they claim.

The Southern Baptist church apologized for the evil that they previously taught against those with hue intact, yet again they find themselves on the side of evil without remorse. Using abortion as a rallying cry, claiming to protect the lives of the unborn and then seeing in real life what is done to those born, shows the truth of the lie that they care not for the innocent babies. They care not for a baby in the womb but only use it as a pretense to claim pro-life when what they truly believe, as shown by other actions, is pro death.

Creating communities of very low income where no one has means of helping others up, keeps them working for low wages, keeps them working more than one job, and often leads them to doing things done only in desperation. America is pro-birth but never pro-life. The life we afford people is our truth about pro-life. If we want to find favor with God, we must turn from our evil ways. We had a congresswoman who slept on the stairs to draw attention to the lifting of the moratorium against renters being evicted. No one joined her until one came the next day, after it had already been lifted. To not take a vote because one didn't think they had enough to win was simply a losers/losing strategy.

Showing who supported life versus death for people would have forced some to vote for it, because they like to shield themselves from the truth of the greed that makes every decision for them. Examine the excuses that they give us and determine if they hold water in the light of day. I pray for God's forgiveness over my life also and if He desires for us to open our home to a family that is now or soon to be homeless, He will direct us. Here I am almost in tears because I'm torn. I recognize that all people haven't had my opportunities and I should be doing more to mentor. I have not done a good job of explaining myself so that people understand where and why I take a stand on certain things. Lord, help me to do better! (Selah).

A day of remorse because I don't want anyone living with us. Thank God, he provided an extension of the moratorium for evictions until October. Will I still feel guilty? Truly I know not. I will certainly try not to justify it by my charitable giving, but I come up at a loss at my selfishness and not desiring to share our home. I always say it's God's house, but the situation showed me that in my heart of hearts I am the one to claim it.

Anyway, I know I'm not perfect; yet I'm still being perfected. God has been so good to us that I don't want to fail him in any way, yet I did, and may well again. Does my sin in not responding to a need that I saw absolve you of your sin that you appear to be blind to? Notice I put my, not ours, for my own wicked heart always reveals itself to a believer.

The same goes for the insurrectionists. If they are Christians, our God will tap them in the heart and ask for an examination and a rededication. Another responding officer committed suicide yesterday. My heart breaks for him because he must have believed that he would be protected, though it hadn't been reported that he held the same beliefs as many of those insurrectionists. Somehow believing that the presidential race was stolen, which it never was, may have had some bearing on his choice. I wonder why the liars aren't being prosecuted by states and even individuals like myself who are living in unsafe conditions because of the lies. There are grifting people for more and more money and money appears to be the end game.

Trump's desperation due to how they are closing in on his evil has him so full of fear now that we just don't know what else will happen. One of his supporters severely beat up a neighbor for having a Biden sign in his yard. If a minor sign can evoke that level of anger to bring violence, how much more will the things that Trump tells them to do as his desperation grows. He was truly the one to get thousands of people to go to the capital to "stop the steal", though there was no steal. How could they stop what was purportedly the steal unless they went into the Capital and in Trump's word "Fight like hell or you won't have a country".

Media like Facebook, Fox, Newsmax, and some more established conservative newscasters in print and on TV are all guilty of the carnage we saw on January 6, 2021, and the carnage we will see next. Trump was asked why he didn't encourage his supporters to take the vaccine and he responded that he didn't want to help Joe Biden. What depth of depravity is willing to kill hundreds of thousands of people who support him to try to make Biden a failure? Though Biden's projection of 70% wasn't reached on July 4th, it was reached less than a month later, even with Republicans and Trump doing all they could to prevent it. It is so sad that human life means so very little to those who are asking for the overthrow of Roe vs. Wade.

If human life out of the womb means so little, then human life in the womb means even less. They fool themselves by claiming that they are protecting babies in the womb, yet after birth, right after birth, they refuse to provide the essential elements of life. They vote against anything that would have a positive quality of life for children after they are born. How does one live in such a demented state of belief that God does not see through the ruse? (Selah)

Trump, as president, caused much turmoil in the USA. They blame it on President Obama who was a Christian man of God, who talked and walked his Christianity, and yet was rejected by the so-called Christian Right. Though they claim otherwise, it was his hue that made it so difficult for them to accept him. A true God man rejected, and a charlatan accepted and even deified. That shows the sickness of the USA and yet they don't want us to teach the truth about racism. It is not to keep the hueloss from feeling guilty, but instead it is so they can continue to keep the lie going that they made America the great country that it is known to be.

Because of the consternation of BLM people are being lied to that others want to displace the hueloss and replace them with the hued. If people don't know the truth about systemic racism that has caused the difficult plight of a group of people, they can continue spewing lies and accepting the law that the hueloss are somehow greater. Remember, if we created laws that were against the hueloss as we created laws against the hued, we could create a climate of hate against the hueloss as has been done against the hued.

Obama is still viewed as a successful president and as a much-admired man but because of his hue, the hueloss became so indignant that they chose a man of satan next because he pretended to want to know Christ. <u>Remember how he held up the Bible!</u> He thinks of himself as a god and racists support him as such, because he is himself racist. You would think that they would see through the ruse, yet they continue to buy into the grift. Ticket sales for events are not doing well so they come up with another way to grift people and the people being grifted don't seem to ever catch on.

I wonder if we are seeing people who are mentally deficient as the biggest supporters, or are they just that racist. It's truly difficult to tell if his people are so dumb that they believe his lies; or if the idea that he can make the hueloss the totally dominant group of people once again is their purpose. God sits high and looks low and sees the evil that his churches, pastors and so-called prophets have wrought with Trump, and He is not pleased.

A day of reckoning is nigh. They have created a climate sure to bring death to their own children thinking that COVID will still only kill black and brown people. God knows the true heart of men like DeSantis, Carlson, Cruz, Abbot and Hannity as well as Trump. Pray that they find God along the way and repent, turning from their evil ways so that their eternity is with God rather than satan. How sad to say you believe in God and in Christ yet serve satan fully. How can they not see truth and know truth when the spirit of truth speaks truth to us? Some things may not be meant to be understood (Selah).

Ezekiel 17:22 The Lord says:" I myself will take a shoot from the very top of a cedar and plant it...(24) All the trees of the forest will know that I the Lord bring down the tall tree and make the low trees grow tall. I, the Lord dry up the green tree and make the dry tree flourish." The tall tree is those who think they are better than others and the shoot is those who have been ruled over unjustly.

Some cultures will never value stuff and power over people. Some believe the land belongs to God, so we all share it. Africa with diamonds and gold has so much wealth that it can be shared.

But look at what happened. Instead of sharing, hueloss people went in and captured diamond mines and keep them in storage to make them cost more, due to the lie that they aren't plentiful. People spend a year's wages on a diamond which may have been picked up from the sand by workers of darker hues being given a penance and the hueloss keeping the money. It must be the Cain spirit that compels some people toward greed, jealousy, competition, lies, and the many evils that we can't even understand. My heart breaks for them for they are no better than my hued brothers and sisters who have the Cain spirit of rage. I guess the Cain spirit can account for anything and everything evil that exists.

Though Adam and Eve were put out of the garden of Eden, their sin didn't stop with them. Today we see young children being taught to hate at an early age. I read where two hueloss boys put a rope around a hued boy's neck to pretend to hang him. That kind of evil is taught and promoted today because hued people are now thought of as uppity because of the demand for equal rights. Not greater rights, but justice and equality. Yet the hueloss feel grievance toward these demands because they don't know the true history of the US and continue to be taught lies that foster hatred yet make them feel superior.

When I speak truth, I am viewed as a rabble-rouser who speaks division. Truth is the only thing that will finally bring us together because truth is of God; and lies will always be the way of satan and his followers. You can pretend with man, but never can you pretend with God. Telling those who follow that evil that satan is responsible for lies, they respect it and me for speaking truth that they don't want to believe.

It has been frightening and yet amazing to see how people that I've known through the years hated President Obama so much that they refer to him as the Antichrist, yet the same ones accepted and supported Trump as a Christian, though during his entire life he has been a fraudulent grifter. So many who claim Christ giving Trump support makes me wonder what they have been taught as Christians. How satan was able to claim the minds and hearts of so many who claim Christ is truly a heartbreaking experience.

I just pray that my hueloss brothers and sisters will listen to the God prompts that I know are being sent so that they can turn from their evil ways before it is too late. I wonder if in fact it's already too late, for they support every lie that Trump brings forth, which is truly sad. When we take ownership of our own unchristian thinking and behavior, then we may be able to promote healing in relationships by active facilitation. Our country must choose to facilitate this healing, not by ignoring or pretending a different truth, but by embracing the truth and repenting of that truth.

Denying the truth hurts much more. For when my truth is denied then the offense is heightened rather than diminished. It's almost as if it doesn't matter that you offend me; but it only matters that I don't offend you with the truth because the truth makes you feel bad. Those who try to get us to recognize and deal with the truth may want you to feel bad in the belief that it may lead you to repentance. Is that really a bad thing?

I know that many people today in America no longer want to whitewash the truth of the evils and perils of slavery and racism in our country. People don't hate America, but they desire that America becomes all that it has promised to become. If we cover up by not teaching truth, believing that we can somehow be absolved of that truth, then we continue the pattern of exploitative racism. We are seeing far too many examples of overt racism again to believe that we don't need to confront the evil before us.

O ur hearts remain deceptive, and we end up in unhealthy relations internally and externally. Fox News network has become a voice of sedition and is allowed to continue because the evil being exposed is done by the entertainers not by their reporters. The evil that they are spewing is having very negative consequences, yet the show must go on.

Tucker Carlson and Hannity both belong in jail for their lies and misinformation, yet the climate in America today of their value in bringing in revenue accords them not just safety from jail but wide acclaim around the world for the evil that they spew. Only God can help us. Yet the places we go to seek God too often are doing the same as Fox News. They report anything from a person of color as a negative, even if it is simply the truth, and then spin it with a hatred of America for saying that truth. We can speak truth about the ugliness of America's past and present and still love America. When you pair truth of America with hatred for America then you are saying that the truth of America is so horrendous that it must be hidden.

The hueloss don't even realize that they too are African Americans, because they have been constantly and consistently lied to. So many believe that they are somehow inherently superior to others. This should be a great warning for any people of God to believe such. It's as though they read only certain parts of the Bible and just dismiss others or have preachers who pick and choose certain passages to produce a different theology, while declaring it's in the word. Yes, "it is in the word" but not as they are presenting it. We are cautioned by that very Bible to study to show ourselves approved; but most of us simply listen to others rather than study to know the truth.

I pray that we embrace our truth and repent of it before it's too late. I don't want to have any hueloss brothers and sisters see me leave with Jesus and they are left behind because they refuse to acknowledge truth and therefore refuse repentance. God loves us all and, because He loved, I love. Even those who hate me, I must love. It's easy to love those who hate me, when I know how much the Lord loves me. (Selah)

Loss will never be greater unless it is for the greater good. Those who lost their hue after leaving Africa long ago should never claim superiority over those who still have it. Family units that left Africa thousands of years ago should not be expected to maintain their hue in colder climates. Even in a place like England that doesn't get a lot of sunny days, the sun can in no way maintain the hue due to lack of activation of melanin. Because we don't teach children that God created man in Africa, which science and the Bible both agree, the ignorance causes some to claim their loss of hue as a superior feature. How can a loss be superior? Does it even make sense to think such? The hueloss may know this instinctively or in observation that giving the hued ones an equal chance means they will achieve more.

I pray that my hueloss brothers and sisters will open their hearts, come before the Lord, and express the fear that consumes them. May they remember that fear is always from satan, never God. Satan, being full of lies, uses the fear to develop that Cain immorality that comes from fear. The lies that they put forth and are believed and only due to fear. No one with real connection to the Lord will believe such, yet we see millions, due to fear, are captured in the rage and soon the ravages of fear due to lies. (Selah).

Ezekiel 24:14 I "The Lord has spoken. The time has come for me to act. I will not hold back, I will not have pity, nor will I relent. You will be judged according to your conduct and actions." God declares His judgment in His time, based on our conduct. Our actions from evil beliefs can often bring forth His wrath. I not only believe in the love of God, but also believe that He is my avenger. For He says vengeance is His.

I will not avenge myself, but I've seen far too often how those who have maligned me have suffered severe consequences, none of which I had wished upon them. I will never have a problem in praying for anyone who counts me as an enemy. Though they will never be my enemy, if I am theirs, I pray for them. Our merciful prayers are accepted by the Lord because of His love for us. We don't even know all that may be done against us, but if it's even one small slight then we know He may repay. Prayers for forgiveness and mercy avail much before God for us and those who claim us as enemies. I believe that this COVID plague may be in response to our need to repent. As we look around the world, we see it's not just a U.S. problem but a world problem. We also see the fires and floods throughout the world like never before. I pray that we take heed of what God is showing us and speaking to us. I know that I am more careful to reflect on my own behavior and how I may be a part of the problem and ask God to show me how to be part of the solution.

20

Repentance is so necessary, for it offers the clarity of action we need to take. We often don't hear from God because of the junk in our own hearts and minds, so that even if He tries to avail us, it can't get through the muck and mire. God in His grace and mercy shows us how they both are so essential to love. Our grace and mercy likewise showcase our love. So many talk about love for God, but I've come to realize that I can't love vertically unless I'm loving horizontally, particularly those who hold me in low esteem. I pray for my brothers and sisters who believe they belong to Christ that they may come to know Him in truth. We are being tested in our faith. Will we follow satan with lies and conspiracy theories or follow God with the truth of his Word and Spirit that help us discern truth? Nothing is hidden from us. It is revealed repeatedly in the word of God. He allows things to happen and at times the negative things may be more detrimental to certain groups of people.

I believe in my heart of hearts that that it was known that black and brown people would suffer the brunt of the devastation of COVID, yet because some leaders didn't know God, they didn't realize that God would bring them to the very edge of death. It's so sad that they used it as an example to ply even more lies about COVID. What an awful waste of life. They are now using the Hitler playbook to engage in even worse behavior. Moving further from God rather than letting that near-death experience of self and death of loved ones to draw them closer to the Lord. Still grifting, still lying, still thinking they won't pay the price. I don't want to pray for such evil ones, but as a child of God I am compelled to pray for them, also.

Never have I seen the level of evil in man as I see in those today. I pray that I also know that our Lord will repay them for his evil. I pray for their repentance because no soul does my God desire to be lost and they are truly lost souls. God continues to pull us to Him through both good and bad. Evangelicals have mastered the art of lying to themselves with their firm stand against abortion and yet refuse to address the very things that the Lord specifically said for us to do, as his followers.

If I keep you from getting rid of a baby in the womb, force you to birth it and then make sure that you have no means to care for the baby physically, emotionally, and spiritually, have I not murdered that baby once out of the womb. It's time to get real. Such love for a baby in the womb and such hatred for the one with the womb to carry the baby makes no sense, yet they still won't see the error of their way. They will force migrants to travel from southern countries and force them to stay in Mexico when they attempt to travel to the U.S. for a chance at a new life. Europeans forget that they traveled here for the same reasons and some of them were murderers, rapists, drug dealers and all kinds of criminals just as people are from every country.

We have never labeled all the people with what a few people of any group do. So is it the locale from which they come or the hue of their skin that causes people to say they love God, yet hate them? We need to check in with God more often, asking that he show us the truth about ourselves. Seeking renewal of the spirit daily is necessary to become and stay grounded in the one who we claim to love and trust. When it's necessary for you to change Jesus from a man of hue to a hueloss one, then truly you have lost Him. The very actions He asked us to take in communion with all men are the things most likely ignored.

This tells us much about ourselves. Who are we when we judge a person by their hue? We don't even get an opportunity to learn their character. Anything that is done that is negative by a person of hue is then applied to all people of that hue. Martin Luther King Jr. declared that he wanted his children to be judged by their character, not by the color of their skin; and today, people have shown their utter lack of comprehending such a small straightforward way of thinking. When one is called out for mischaracterizing what he said, they are offended and respond in even more evil ways. BLM has never been antifa and even if it were, it would be a good thing.

Antifascism became active under Trump because they knew that he was a totalitarian fascist wannabe by the very definition of a fascist. Seeing the numbers of people who were supporting his fascism had to show alarm. Most of us didn't know of the organization called antifa, if there is even such a thing. Associating them with BLM does injury to both. Both groups are attempting to protect that which needs protection, black lives from being killed by police because of their hue and trying to keep America a democratic republic rather than a fascist totalitarian country. Both were viewed and labeled as bad.

Why would politicians connect BLM and antifa as if they were one and the same? For one useful reason. Both could then be viewed as negative, mostly to take away support for BLM. I wonder today if the hueloss supremacists are using antifa to bring negativity to BLM by association though there is no association. I now see hueloss head coverings in black w/white lettering of antifa on the side of the head coverings. People questioned if they even existed, so why would they now, having been scorned, come out with such. Masterful use of an evil mind to incite fear in the hearts of the ignorant perhaps?

Ezekiel 33:31- My people come to you...Their mouths speak of love, but their hearts are greedy for unjust gain. How the Evangelical of America got caught in such a trap of foolishness is beyond me. I don't even believe that hatred of hue is primary, but they fear the loss of continued unjust gain.

21

The mouths that speak of love and justice for unborn babies speak more of fear of loss of status if hued people are given equal rights. Many states are now enacting laws that make it more difficult for those of color to vote, which is a fundamental right in America. They are also enacting new laws that give Republicans the right to overthrow votes in their states. They are already throwing out millions of those on the voting rolls, which someone of great stupidity somehow believes that those people were illegally allowed to vote. Supporters of the lie/lies also spew that garbage. Ignorance is not bliss for the ignorant nor for those who must suffer consequences of the lies.

Simone Biles stated that she is pro-choice because of what she suffered personally in foster care. So many people do foster care to pad their income so that they can have gain for self at the children's expense. Those who are against a woman having a choice of carrying a baby to term or not, easily say to give the baby up for adoption without understanding that most black and brown hued babies will age out of foster care if they survive to that age rather than be adopted.

Hueloss people often see things so very differently because of personal experience. The hued child has a vastly different life than the hueloss one. Most parents seeking to adopt are hueloss and they desire hueloss babies. Unfortunately, the hued babies get a chance to experience molestation, abandonment issues, neglect, malnutrition, and many other ills that hueloss don't have to experience that often comes with being in foster care. I believe in a quality of life that God desires, so I also believe in pro-choice. Not so much because of the ills of foster care, but for a woman's right to decide what happens to her body.

Right now, many Republican lawyers are asking the Supreme Court to use the 14th amendment to overturn Roe vs. Wade that could outlaw abortions even before a heartbeat of the baby is in the womb. How do we take away a woman's right to decide what happens to her body on the claim that the baby's right to life takes precedence over a woman's right to decide the ultimate choice of her body?

I only know one person who has talked with me about their abortion experience. They acknowledge deep regret in taking a life yet recognized that their circumstances left them with little alternative. Pregnant in youth, she married the father, graduated from high school and went to college. Lo and behold, she ends up pregnant once again.

She could deny the first child a possible decent life or deny the unborn child life. She felt she would have to drop out of college, which was already exceedingly difficult with one child and would be impossible with two. She made the decision to abort and always regretted it, yet she knows she made the better choice for her family.

Some forbid the use of birth control on religious grounds, just as the Right to Life groups are attempting to do after they overturn Roe vs. Wade. Birth-control use often causes spontaneous abortion before it can be determined that a baby is already forming because it brings on the menses that expels the baby. Many so called right to lifers don't even know that this is the agenda. Is a life less precious at two weeks vs two months? We must get real with ourselves and look at the rights we are trampling on as we try to claim rights for the unborn. (Selah).

A quote by Tacitus born in AD 56 made some provocative statements. One such statement was "it belongs to human nature to hate those you have injured". How appropriate to examine that, considering what is now happening in the U.S. They just enacted a law against the teaching of CRT, a construct of thought to show how slavery and the consistent racism has shaped America's racist policy from slavery, to segregation, to passing of Social Security, to redlining, to payment of money to football players for traumatic brain injuries, to the handcuffing of a black real estate agent and his clients for being in a home, to the claim by a "Karen" that she was the victim when she called the police on the black birdwatcher claiming he had threatened her because he wanted her to put her dog on a leash. So many more, such as the choice of location approval by the government for the location of industries that spew toxic chemicals, to inequity of school funds, too low appraisal prices of homes in black communities yet with higher rates of taxation though fewer services.

And let's not forget the differences in policing. Black men/ boys stopped because of having a scented piece of cardboard from the car wash hanging from their mirror and being killed for it. The fear of the truth shows what should be taught, not what should continue to be kept in the dark..

The racist strategies that are still being used today to present U.S. as a non-racist country are astounding. The U.S. is a racist country founded on principles of racism from before the constitution was even written. Instead of lying about what we were and are, we need to embrace our past so that we can move on to a better future. Yet as Tacitus said, "human nature hates those that we've injured." The hueloss of America know that they've given injury after injury to people of hue. They are consistently enacting laws against the right to vote so that they control all the laws.

We need to change direction, not forbidding the teaching of CRT, which is only taught in graduate school anyway since it is but one construct of explanation. We should instead simply teach the truth and choose to repent of that truth that makes us uncomfortable. That's the only way for us to embrace real change. People like the "white supremacist" by their various names will not hate people of color if they recognize that they too are people of color from Africa who have simply lost their darker hues.

Again, we are all African Americans. We can't get around that and God is not pleased with our continued evil actions. We need to see the plague as God speaking to us. It was known and told to our leaders that COVID would be very harmful to people of color, yet in their callous disregard for those people, they let COVID claim the lives of 6000 people, most of whom were people of color. Now that it's impacting more hueloss who are their supporters, some still won't encourage them to get vaccines because they won't do anything to help Joe Biden. How sad that people who call themselves by Christ's name have been unable to see through the ruse. They and their media supporters have wreaked havoc on our land. The insurrectionists have been given short sentences and low fines, yet we still pretend that the USA is not a racist country (Selah).

23

O f all the beautiful songs about America, why choose the one that is truly racist, written as the enslaved were fighting with the hueloss, not for their direct freedom but for America. It's further evidence that the intent is to keep America divided so the rich and powerful can exploit those hueloss to hate those whose melanin is still evident. We must change if we want to have many tomorrows. They are talking about and planning for another civil war to put Trump back in office. He is even calling for massive protests if he gets indicted for any of his many illegal activities. He does not want to have to face the consequences of his deeds of cheating and now it may be time to pay the piper. He wants to continue keeping it a secret from the ignorant that he is a failed businessman with little appetite for anything but grifting, lying, cheating, and manipulating people. Sounds a lot like satan to me.

We need to recognize that when athletes don't stand for the flag or the anthem, it does not show hatred of America but a very strong love for what America is supposed to represent. When we fail and they show their disappointment that the flag and the anthem are lies to people of color, why not show anger that we as a people of America have continued to fall so far short of the ideals of America. Disappointment in America is not hatred of America. You can be disappointed in people and not hate them.

I think the hueloss use media to bring more contention. Trump has been elevated as the catalyst of racial hatred because he was willing to use destructive means of the country for his personal power. He's just like Hitler, when the fighting that he caused started, he ran away and hid. Appropriate for the coward that he was and appropriate too for the coward that he is now. It amazes me that I'm one of the few who believes in democracy so much that a presidential run for him in2024 is absolutely absurd, for I strongly believe that he will be in jail or will have escaped to another country. Trump, thy name is treason.

My heart still breaks for those who have become emboldened to voice their hatred toward people of darker hues. They somehow forget that our God is on the throne, and He shares his throne with no one and definitely not with one that is engaged with satan as a partner. Though I try to fear not because God is Alpha, Omega, and all in between, it's hard not to believe that his hueloss followers could start a war between what they call races. How ridiculous to think that they would give up democracy for such. Those who claim Christ must renounce evil and repent of their fear and racist actions. Lord, please forgive them when they repent. Repent not just of actions but of the evil thoughts that brought about such actions.

God shares his throne with no one and we as his people should never put a mere mortal on the throne with God. I have hope for America because even though Biden was one who showed racism at one time, he turned his heart to God and was able to repent of his evil. Repentance can only come when we recognize our behavior as evil and desire to be reunited with God through the process of that repentance. I thank God that many of our hueloss brothers and sisters have already done so. Fox News and the like recognize this and felt that they had to be the voice to bring division, yet they claim to love democracy.

It becomes clearer and clearer that it's all about their god, which is money, power, or both. I look at some of the hued ones who support them and readily say that America is not a racist country. They do it for money and power because no one can be so emotionally or mentally damaged having lived life as a hued person not to have experienced time and again the impact of a hueloss sense of anger at them just for taking up space as a person of color.

Even young children of color experience things to show that America is racist, though it shouldn't be since we are all African Americans in the USA. The Lord is the source of our strength and our salvation; and though my spirit grieves what I see happening to our country, I trust God to end it or help us go through it. All the evil that has been done to the hued people of the USA, God has been a witness to it and is not pleased. He works in the heart of the hued to forgive repeatedly and he continues to work in the hearts and minds of some of the hueloss so they will not continue hating. For truly there is no reason to hate except for fear. If you operate from fear, then you are serving satan, not God, for He has not given us the spirit of fear.

Those persons justifying all manner of evil based on lies are guilty, but so are the perpetrators of the lies. QAnon caused a man to kill his two young children. Though he was the killer and will be held responsible, the ones who have perpetuated this fraudulent belief system will all be held guilty as well. The more they do to strip power from those who believe in equal rights for all mankind, the stronger they will become because God is on their side.

When God spoke of some being worse than Sodom, it had nothing to do with sex but instead the withholding of care and justice for others. How He must be disappointed with us when He sees the evil that is being spewed forth. So many of Trump's followers of wealth and privilege know better, yet they continue along the line of lies to raise money from the poor and gullible. It may be a good money-maker but all of it will blow up in their faces. To Carlson, Hannity, Bannon, Miller, Jr., Eric, Ivanka, Owens, etc., God is displeased, and you will soon meet your just reward from Him because you are following satan. I pray that some of you will publicly repent before the people.

24

I always knew that the popular online means of communicating with others was to be evil because it was only done for wealth. They enable people to attack others for reason or no reason. They are the greatest perpetrators of the lies that are causing great division, not just along the lines of what is called race, but class, politics and any area in which divisiveness can be used to generate finances. The wickedness of the hearts of man today in big and small ways makes me want Jesus to return soon, yet I know that it will not be in my will but His will. I pray for these unrepentant who think that because I speak truth from the word of God that I am being divisive and yet that is what God expects from each of us. How heartless is the one who judges me evil because I give them the truth of the word of God, which they claim to believe yet are so caught up in lies that no truth can anymore be found in them. My heart hurts because they think they are true believers. (Selah)

Most people think that the hueloss have accepted slavery of others as their God-given right, but I believe wholeheartedly that the guilt felt as given by the Holy Spirit has been such that they had to carve out a rationale and propagate it among the masses of the hueloss to help salve their conscious. To mistreat someone or something we must somehow rationalize and magnify any overt differences to make it appear that there is an inherent difference, which God has created to justify taking advantage of another. It's so easy to lie to oneself to justify evil, but that doesn't work forever.

Even when they are spewing forth words of hatred to self and others, it's merely a means by which they reinforce the lies that satan has given them as justification for the evil said and done. Their desire in doing the evil is to feel better about it; for in claiming the name of Jesus, you automatically get Holy Spirit and the Spirit reveals truth to us. Even when pastors preach justification of evil, they know that is indeed evil. So in order to ward off the pain of willful sin against the Lord, we shrug off the feelings of guilt and keep telling ourselves the lies that we've been fed, or we leave the churches that feed us lies.

Many of the famous church leaders of the hueloss are upset that their children are no longer in their churches. They blame others for this, not recognizing that it is themselves. Without segregation the lies no longer hold true. Parents and church leaders are increasingly saddened by the relationships of their hueloss children with children of still hued. Though some may enter these relationships to have financial gain from the hued, often it is because of love that the relationships are changing. How does one look upon your own flesh and blood who are hued and still hate. I know some still do, but now they are few, rather than many. When I saw this happening more and more, I realized that our Lord was at work to bring about the change that America needed. Trying to hold onto racist, elitist ideas and ideals can no longer work. As they see this ideation changing, they go to another tactic. Now they want hueloss men to dominate the hueloss women in order to control who they can date and marry. Some are even saying now that hueloss females should not have the vote since they found that too many of them didn't support Trump.

To deign to suppress people to achieve evil objectives will only bring forth the wrath of our Lord on their heads. But how do we help them see this? Love by man for mankind is truly not enough. They need a touch by the Lord. I pray and expect to hear of preachers falling on their knees in the pulpits of America and stating the evil that has blocked their love for so long, and they are now repenting of that evil. For anyone who truly knows God has His heart and can see through a manipulating grifter who sows discord for the sake of lining his own pockets.

Yet even they are not the Antichrist as some say. Time has not come yet for Jesus' return though most yearn for it and claim it. I, however, feel it is arrogant to believe that I can tell the time when our Lord clearly says that even he didn't and only the Father knew the time. Remember they have been claiming it's time ever since Jesus died and yet these thousands of years have not changed the minds of the deluded to understand that they know not. It is too important a subject to play with but play with it they do. Fame and gain is the name of the game; and by any means necessary, they are willing to engage in order to achieve the fame and financial gain that actually means so very little. (Selah)

25

Our behavior toward others demonstrates the truth of the belief that we have in the Lord. If you hate other humans that you don't even know because of negative beliefs about skin hues, then you certainly can't truly love the one you claim to love. To love God vertically, we must love man horizontally. That's made clear from the Old to the New Testament. We fool ourselves if we claim otherwise. Our God sits high, looks low, and enters the affairs of mankind to bring about His desires for the world. No matter how much the hueloss mistreat the hued, never will you find overall hatred against anyone for mistreatment. I count not lost anything I've been denied but I count it gain that God provides, restores, and keeps me. I understand the concept of being struck on the cheek and offering the other cheek. Not that I truly want or will even let someone hit me, but the evil inflicted against me will still allow me to help someone else.

I used to strike back against any injury. Even asking a senior hueloss friend why she had to make Jesus 'white' to worship Him. The ancestry companies could provide an excellent service that helps reconciliation among ethnic groups. Instead of allowing people to check the box not to receive the info of African roots after the uprising against finding out 2-15% of African lineage, giving that information would show how most everyone in the U.S. has same mixture of what ethnic groups they belong to and show "white supremacists" that they 1.) are not white since whiteness is a construct much like CRT and 2.) we are a nation that is already ethnically diverse and therefore no need for the alarm.

If no one is "white" how could there be "white supremacy"? It could not exist and should not exist. Given what the US is going through now, trying to show how evil and heartless the hueloss are, doing away with black and white would pave the way to some other construct rather than a divisive one. The truth of the Bible, when explained properly, can be called "divisive". You may wonder how truth can be called "divisive". Actually, it can't be but those who don't like the truth just consider it so. How sad a society that settles for feel good lies over the truth of God's word. I'm stumped by such evaluation.

Truth is what God gives us. Satan is always the one behind the lies. I have wondered how in the world millions of people could believe an election was stolen, even though they themselves voted against the person. Just because the fervency of one candidate causes people to ignore the health warnings, doesn't mean a candidate is popular in ideology. One idea may have been the driving card-racism while that same thing may have caused far more to reject that evil. God sits high and looks low and will always have a winning edge among His creation.

Remember, satan is a created being just as we are so he has limited powers. His power is spread by evil while God's power is spread by love. Love wins out against evil every time. Evil seems to be vastly accepted right now, but in time it must fall because our God wills it so. This is an opportunity to show man his depravity. Take January 6, 2021, could any of us have thought that the likes of such could happen? Absolutely not. How about generals even now telling people that they have rights to fight to take back a country that they never had. America is for all of us, not the few who believe that they are hueless rather than hueloss. It's a sad day in America when money stands out so visibly as the goal of those seeking powerful positions. Anytime that is the motivation, then we can tell readily that satan is the one who they are serving. It's amazing that they don't easily recognize this themselves. (Selah).

Race is now in the bible referring to people, but it was not always so. Race came into use during the slave trade, for those involved had to create a justification for enslaving people. Europeans used to be Europeans in name rather than "white". Italians and Spaniards were looked down upon within the European community due to their mixture with Africa, yet they did not call themselves "white". When it became necessary to reclassify the hued as a lesser form of man, then "white" began to be used for Europeans so that they could justify the subjugation of others.

So began the evil that we see today called "white supremacy" whether by Hitler or others with the same devastating results. The aim to gain followers by any means necessary has been the game plan all the time. The real aim is to use divisive means to gain more wealth and power. America has never repented of its shame, so they continue finding ways and means to denigrate those that they so evilly used as property; and had the audacity to use the Bible to support their lies.

S lavery in the Bible was never the type of slavery in America. Look at how they were brought from their native lands. Bound together in the bowels of ships with room only to lie or sit, in some cases. Given limited food because, even though chained, the fear was that one could overtake many of the hueloss. Because they still worked in hard labor on lands in Africa, they remained strong. If they had to relieve themselves of bodily waste, whether solid or liquid they had to do it as they were stripped naked for all to see and could not even have the dignity of private waste letting. If food became scarce on the boats return voyage, they threw the enslaved overboard to save food for the workers on the slave ships. Their poor planning led them to file for the insurance for the loss of those that they had enslaved when they reached port. Fortunately, this is how we know of some of the worst actions of the enslavers. The hueloss today tend to declare that the Africans sold other Africans into slavery, which was true on only a limited basis. It's sad that the evil mind of some put the blame for their lust, greed, and inhumane trafficking in human beings on others rather than repenting of what their forebears have done.

If my parents' actions have caused negative consequences for any person, then as a believer of Christ I must, at the very least, own that they did the evil and repent of it since my forebears did not. If we refute and refuse truth, we will remain a nation divided. Our younger hueloss population don't see the hued in the negative way that their forbears do and many churches of the hueloss are losing their population of young people. The audacity is to blame the hued even for this rather than accepting that their children don't suffer the same racism that they do.

Fox News has become as racist as the people to whom they cater. They blame Obama becoming president as a justification for their rise of racism. Remember however, racism couldn't rise unless it was already there. To take offense to a "black man" being in the White House that "black men" built is an affront to all sensibilities. Today it's readily said that Obama released the racism of today. He released no such thing. The idea of a black president was just so offensive to the evil of some hueloss that they created every myth that is attached to him today.

One of my friends and her church were so offended that she knew for a fact that Jesus was returning before she died. The thinking that he would return for such evil-minded persons is appalling to me, yet they see no fracture in hating hued people and claiming to love the Lord. She even believed Jesus had to be "white", though no such entity existed at that time. The idea of a Jesus of color/hued was so offensive that they had to create a blonde/blue-eyed figure to represent a brown skin, brown-eyed man. Look at the movies about African people of fame. They were all represented in movies as "white", yet they never have been. (Selah)

Jeremiah 23:10b-12 The prophets follow an evil course and use their power unjustly. Both prophet and priest are godless. Even in my temple, I find their wickedness, declares the Lord. Therefore, their path will become slippery, they will be banished to darkness and there they will fall. 13:b-"They prophesied by Baal and led my people astray." 14b "They Strengthen the hands of evil doers so that not one of them turns from their wickedness."

27

Too often, we look not back at the word of God on a regular basis so we can attain understanding of what's happening today. Evil times come around periodically, and the evil leaders bring the evil times. God uses these evil leaders to teach us to recognize Him from the evil ones. If your preacher attests to things against the word or manipulates the word to verify his evil then know that he is sent by satan, not by God. How easily so many were duped by those who were sent by satan, I'll never understand. The spirit of satan in them is the only thing that could align them with the evil doers. Some people believe that it is OK for them to hate groups of people who look different yet are truly children of God. The love of God may change some hearts, but most will remain rigidly tied to the evil of hatred. God sits high and looks low and is displeased at what He sees. He sees the racist behavior as worse than Sodomites showing that He places great value on how we treat one another.

We can go to church, sing praises to God, put in an offering, take communion, all in a pretense of having a relationship with Christ Jesus, yet continue with hatred in our hearts. We can fool man, sometimes, but we can never fool God. If we are His, He will show us the truth of ourselves for those who truly belong to Him will hear his voice of conviction. Those that belong to satan don't hear God and will keep their hearts, minds, ears and eyes bent to satan and happily follow him who delights in their destruction. For the end will be their destruction.

My soul cries out for the destruction of the innocent who get caught up in the crosshairs of evil because of their relationship with the evil doers. Many young people today lament about their parents being caught up in QAnon which readily shows how contaminating evil truly is. There is no Q, yet people continue believing in such to the degree that they even kill the innocent in the name of Q belief. How abhorrent is it that a father would kill his innocent children based on conspiracies put forth by this malignant group? The political arena today is so divisive that one group who shows themselves as truly evil are revered by the so called "Christians" at the same time. "So called" because one can't be a follower of satan and be a Christian.

My heart aches at the hardness of heart that they will never risk the death of their own children by a disease that hits those communities of color harder. Only when the hueloss children start dying at a rate higher than communities of color will they come to their senses. Governors giving extra money to school districts that don't protect the health of children seems absurd, yet that is what is being done today. The desire to see a Democrat president fail is so great that they put their own children in harm's way. Claiming rights that we don't have as Americans, yet not defending the rights that we are supposed to have. They wonder why their children don't want to be a part of their churches nor do they see the evil that is being taught there. Even if they don't know the bible, they have the Spirit that guides them to the way of understanding, so they leave those churches. In today's climate it's difficult to find a hueloss church that doesn't promote racism, so their children remain churchless.

I truly pray for our hueloss brothers and sisters who abandoned Christ to follow a man who was a deceiver, a thief, a charlatan, a liar, and one of ill repute all his life. What does our God think of that? It has to hurt Him far more than it hurts me, and I am truly hurt as I see those I love making such horrendous choices of support and belief. (Selah)

Daniel 8:12 "Because of rebellion the Lord's people and the daily sacrifice were given over to it. It prospered in everything it did, and truth was thrown to the ground." Evil may prosper for a time, but it only prospers for a time. Time and again it is shown that God places constraints on the evil that He allows, for His desire is that all men will come to Him in repentance and accept Him as Lord and master. If we put ourselves in His place, then never will we recognize our evil and our need for redemption. For our egos will tell us that we are already redeemed though we are the greatest of sinners.

To take a good true look in the mirror cannot be done by our own volition but only under the amazing grace of a God who loves us yet can never demand that we come to him for cleansing. When we ourselves have hearts open to Him, He readily reveals the evil in us through word and deed and leads us into repentance so we can have a right relationship with Him. Only our lack of an open heart and mind to Him keeps us prevailing in the evil that we've adopted.

If both the Bible and science agree that man began in Africa and Africa even today remains having the most natural riches of any place, why is it not taught to our children. Europeans made havoc there, stealing so much of the wealth and meaningful natural resources. The enslaved were also natural resources. The weak were left behind and yet they are blamed for not fighting against the transgressors who came back with the Cain spirit and the hueloss.

To keep the truth from the hueloss, generation after generation has caused them to adopt a lie of superiority and maintain a lie of "white supremacy". No such thing exists. Evil supremacy does exist however and not teaching truth reinforces the lies that the hueloss believe. That may be why the Spirit of God is so weak in them for how can He exist in a space shared with satan? God sits on His throne alone and shares it with no one. Never will He enter those who are serving satan. They must throw satan and the evil aside to make room for God. Let repentance come and draw closer and closer to our Lord so that He can change your vision and your outlook. The hued ones can't be viewed as evil because of a hue. You will then recognize those hued and hueloss who breed contempt and division and you will know how to recognize the true spirit of man. You will be able to tell a charlatan from a true believer and you will no longer call evil good and good evil. (Selah)

The darkness of America seems to hover over the entire world. America must be strong in democracy of human rights as an influence on the rest of the world. Totalitarian governments bring chaos. Though democratic governments can have chaos, they don't use it to justify killings as do totalitarian ones. I praise God that the people of Afghanistan are now marching in the streets against Taliban rule under Saria law. Not only do women count only as sex slaves for husbands and are duty bound to care for house and home exclusively, they also have no voice. Men are given all the rights there as in America, but to a greater disparity. I pray that God will make them continue to march for rights.

Remember the enslaved of America were not given schooling and were not allowed to read. The same will be true in Afghanistan today if we can see how backward-looking that belief in practice was back then; surely, we can see the devastating effect of such today. I pray that we can relocate all who want to leave there. The Taliban will find that they can only fail because only Russia will give them money. It's time for all people to be free. To keep freedom from any is to keep freedom from all. I heard some Republicans say that they need to take back the vote from people of color and from women because they don't know how to vote. After all it was women who gave the victory to Biden. How sad that fear causes the hueloss male to trample on my rights and the rights of all those who believe differently.

I wonder what the supporters don't understand about Trump as a dictator. Those supporters of color, after he is dictator, will have no more rights than I would, nor would the women or the average man. Dictators surround themselves with the rich so that control is maintained at all costs. Even now, they are controlling the vaccine so that their donors and themselves can make money off other medications that don't prevent you from dying when you get Covid.

To kill people for money surely shows that the Republicans are not pro-life which is their claim to fame and gain. Phony religion is not Christianity. They forget that God hates religion. He loves those who love Him not those who pretend to love Him for what they can get from that pretense. Our God sits high and looks low, and the religious evil will be exposed more and more that supports those who are as close to being an antichrist without actually being the antichrist (Selah)

"If my people who are called by my name, will humble themselves and pray, seek my face and turn from their evil ways then I will hear from heaven and will heal their land." The first word "if" makes what our God will do conditioned on what we are to do. My people indicate an expectation that we are His servants because we call ourselves by His name indicating that we've answered the call to Him. Humble ourselves means he insists that our hearts and minds be humbled before Him knowing that we ourselves are nothing without Him.

Prayer is our lifeline to God, and we should pray without ceasing, for a lifeline to Him is our life blood connection. We may keep living physically, but spiritual death is true death and difficult to come back from. Physical death in the Spirit is simply leaving the body yet gaining that spiritual body and being with God eternally. Praying allows God to enter in and direct our steps as we listen to Him respond to us when we pray. As we pray, we are always seeking the will of God for our lives, His will is his face. We can then turn from our evil, wicked ways since we don't always recognize our wickedness. We sometimes call evil good and good evil having lost our steadfast response to God and instead believe the lies of man which causes us to sin in ways that we could never have imagined.

Staying in touch with Him lets us discern true evil and wickedness. Through His word and prayer reinforces what we are to do. Prayer seeking guidance will not be given to us unless we pray in earnest. We are then able to tell the difference between godly good and satanic evil. Our convictions from God lead us to live holy lives in love for others as God lives in love with us. God is a promise-keeper who keeps every one of his promises. So, we can count on the healing of our land in mind and spirit. When our hearts are right before our Lord, He will not fail to hear us, and He is earnest to answer with healing of our land. The most important thing is "if". We too often expect God to do what He has promised without meeting the condition of the "if" requirement. We can see miracles all our lives if we'd live to respond positively to God's "ifs".

Meeting the condition means that we must change our thinking. The hued and hueloss must come together before the Lord in love and forgiveness. In repentance, He will receive our prayers, speak to our hearts, assist us in turning from evil by exposing it so that He can then keep His promises that were predicated on the "if". If, then is so significant with God because He is holy and expects us to also be holy. Some believe everyone is saved. This is a lie from the pit of hell with no truth. People think they can live their lives and escape hell, but the truth is not in them for He speaks to our hearts and lets us know right from wrong. When we choose wrong because the preacher teaches us wrong by manipulating scripture, then we are as evil as they are.

"Study to show thyself approved" puts the study of God's word on us individually if we seek a servant relationship that becomes a son relationship. From servant to son takes love, trust and obedience. To love God is to obey Him. For disobedience shows us who we actually love - satan. Some people give great deference to satan believing that he has so much power. Remember, he was a created being just as we are. His power is what we give him through our lack of love, selfishness, and a host of wicked thinking and evil acts that we don't even think are evil because we have been so bent on evil that we think it's OK. God forgives a repentant heart not a manipulative one. Search your heart for truth. (Selah).

Hosea 4:7-9 "The more preachers there were, the more they sinned against me;" They exchanged their glorious God for something disgraceful. They feed on the sins of my people and relish their wickedness. And it will be like people, like priests. I will punish both of them for their ways and repay them for their deeds. Hosea 6a- "My people are destroyed for the lack of knowledge because you have rejected knowledge." 4:14b "A people without understanding will come to ruin." We have a Gomer in our lives at some time. We are called to give out far more than we think it should cost but because of the call of Christ on our lives, we must view them as priceless as God does, and give more than we even thought we could, and far more than we ever thought we would.

30

I put some of the blame of the racism in America on the preachers who claim their agenda to be the protection of life or pro-life, yet they still give support to ones who paid for abortions and let over 600,000 people die from COVID … and maybe more. They knew that COVID was detrimental to black and brown citizens, so I consider it murder to allow it. Then to propagate that it was essentially like the flu, speaking against masks and vaccinations, holding rallies to spread it more and speaking harshly against those who advocated protective measures.

All of this will be held to account, not by man but by a greater authority who some don't even believe in because they have never been held to account. But even with the preachers' influence on the people, the people themselves are held to account for supporting them. They are no more pro-life than the Republicans that they support. They advocate for the rich under the guise of pro-life, yet they can readily see that the Republicans never support anything that is pro-life but a baby in the womb. I wonder if they realize how adverse their thinking is to pro-life with the low wages, rampart air pollution, with the killing of brown and blacks by the police, with their attitude towards social programs that help the poor and all other administrative efforts to create a more equitable society. "Study to show that self-approved" is totally ignored.

Lord, please convict the hearts of those who sincerely claim your name yet follow blindly that path of evil because their preachers preach and teach the satanic way of interpreting the word of God. We will be held to account for all of the "murders" that occurred under those who are followers for they are just as guilty for the 600,000 plus deaths that are attributed to the leaders. Though my heart goes out to my hueloss brothers and sisters, they too are as guilty as the others for the division in our country at present. How they have tried to deny what happened on January 6, 2021 and placed the blame for the actions on some other than Trump supporters who were sent to the capital to "fight hard or you won't have a country".

You can't "fight" to stop something peacefully. What a joke for anyone to believe that Trump was not responsible for what happened on January 6th or either they think we are fools to believe such. It's frightening to see the level of overt hatred being displayed by the "Karens", male or female who use their privilege against anyone for speaking a language other than English. Americans go to many countries and don't speak the language native to that country with no negative consequences. Yet some Americans expect foreigners in their home countries to speak English; but anyone coming to America, we expect them to speak American English. It's an abomination of privilege to have such a mindset, but events of every day show that it's happening more and more.

Whether these things are done to provoke others to try to force them into negative engagement or the level of privilege is such that they think rules of engagements only apply to the hueloss to be perpetuated on those of hue, it's still a very sordid affair. I pray that people begin listening to God rather than to their preachers, given what is now being taught that causes greater division. There seems to be a tendency to cover up truth in the name of cooperation. If America never repents of her moral abomination to the sin of slavery, she will never heal, and the festering wounds of our country will only grow. It would be so much easier to repent and allow God to heal the divide rather than to let it grow deeper and deeper, generation after generation. When will we say enough is enough? The time is now. We must stop the lies of a steal and of supremacy! (Selah).

Hosea 7:2-3- Tells us that God remembers all our evil deeds. That should be enough to bring us to repentance. Their sins engulf them. They delight the leader with their wickedness. 8:11 Altars for sin offerings have become altars for sinning. Those of privilege having gotten away for so very long with evil may really believe that they will never have to answer for their evil deeds. Unfortunately, the more they get away without payment the more they engage in the action and add even more evil actions to it.

31

God is a God of great patience, but he has called all of us to repentance. He searches the hearts of man, knowing who has a possibility of repentance. Others He knows are too evil to ever repent and He gives them more and more time to do their evil. We may wish that He would act swiftly against those who are so callous, yet because each of us, evil ones included, are His creation, He shows great patience. Though it may be unlikely that some will change because their privilege has been reinforced time and time again, God in his infinite patience is like a mother whose child is on drugs. Time and again they are brought to the brink of destruction and yet never go all the way to their demise. So, they think that each time they can do it again and again until one day there are no more chances, and they die from an overdose.

To the brink and back causes many to believe that they will be rescued every time. Yet, that one time was different, and they are no more. We can only pray that at the very brink of their self-destruction that they repent though God didn't relent this time. It's amazing how often many people repeat this pattern of behavior because their privilege has led them to believe that they will always escape at the last moment. Woe to the person who believes this foolishness. Foolishness to us as believers yet to those who practice satan's ways, it's their reality. I still pray for such persons in the belief that anyone can change, and I am never partial to the inability that God may capture a heart and turn it to Himself. God remembers all our evil deeds, yet He is ever willing to forget them when we come before his throne of grace and mercy in repentance. Some, however, are so engulfed by their sins that they go to their death beds without repentance.

Hell was not created for man, but for satan and the third of the angels that followed him in rebellion to God. Man can choose hell, but hell can never choose man because of the love that God has for us. Those who follow the evil ones in support of, or blindness to the evil are subject to the same fate as the evil one. God specifically says to have no other gods before him, yet people who call themselves Christians have and are following down behind some who personify the evilest in the world. Having made a golden calf of a man, these Christians are exhibiting one of the most callous acts against our Lord, yet, with great zeal they do it. The basics of God worship seem to be lost now in a desire for hueloss reinforcement of what they call "white supremacy". They are proud of their actions, yet we are kept from teaching the truth about those same actions. Now the KKK can no longer be taught as an evil organization but is now to be glorified in 2021. How quickly we have reverted to the old patterns of hate and division based on lies. It's as if we forget who the father of lies is. Remember satan is, always has been, and always will be the father of lies and liars (Selah).

Hosea 10:12 "Sow righteousness for yourselves, reap the fruit of unfailing love and break up unplowed ground, for it is time to seek the Lord until He comes and showers righteousness on you." Some of those who experience religion all their lives remain fallow ground. No teaching, other than what they learned from church and family, will ever be able to penetrate until Holy Spirit begins to speak deeply into their lives. It is past time for those who have been in church for a lifetime to become real Christians. Our God sees through the phoniness of claiming pro-life when they won't even get vaccines so that they can commit no fault murder. Knowing that COVID ravages communities of color far greater than the hueloss and adding to their injury from the plague is murder. They think they do it and no one knows, but it is not only known but eventually a price must be paid for murder.

Be concerned about all life, then God may believe that you are pro-life. Saying you are pro-life is used to garner favor with a god that doesn't exist, believing somehow that it is God almighty. Remember the Lord can see through the ruse. Let's look at all the ways you kill or don't give life to black and brown people. You make sure the worst air pollution/polluters are in their communities that affect them after being brought home from the hospital. You make sure to locate oil pipelines underground in their communities. You rape the public schools for religious and private schools so they can't get an adequate education.

You don't keep drugs from their neighborhoods so mothers and fathers can get hooked trying to escape their horrible circumstances for a short time. The drugs are supplied to those communities by the hueloss, often by those in power positions. The drugs cause parents to neglect or mistreat their children so the children are then taken away and put in foster care. Though some people do foster care as a benevolent gesture others will do it for a malevolent one in which children are used as slaves physically/and or sexually. Putting the parents in jail and charging them with felonies takes away their rights to vote. Should the right to vote be taken away for misdeeds or is jail a sufficient punishment? Even after they serve their sentence, they must come up with money to pay all fines before getting their right to vote back. Why is there even a fine if they receive a jail sentence. That appears to be double jeopardy. Some states may not even allow that. Most of the cheating in voting was done by those voting for the

Republican party, yet black and brown people are the ones who are charged with longer sentences for the mistake of voting when they even have certification that they can vote.

Lies instituted to keep black and brown people from voting keep changing to increase the burdens on people of color. People of color often are unable to post bail and stay in jail for years without trial. Some even commit suicide while waiting for trial. Grocery stores that sell unfit food, yet it's the only food available when you don't have transportation in some communities. Often, it's priced much higher than grocery stores in other communities, but they have no choice but to purchase it, whether rancid or not. It's amazing how the system has been set up to take advantage of people of color even when the claim is made to give them an advantage. They must take out loans to go to for profit institutions that prepare them to take minimum wage jobs and have childcare paid for during their matriculation. But childcare isn't paid for if they go to college to be trained for something that pays a living wage.

32

We keep saying America is not a racist country, but from its very founding, the laws enacted tell a very different story. At present the truth is no longer to be told on the basis "of not making hueloss people feel guilty". What malarkey! They don't feel guilty because those of the hued are labeled by them as lesser people. Using the bible to justify evil may work with man; but it will never work with God. For God knows the heart of man that is sown and shown in how he treats his fellow men of all hues. May our Lord pierce the heart of those who lie mightily to themselves that they are Christians by showing them truth by shining the light on their thoughts and actions.

Holy Spirit, speak to their hearts so that they can move away from the lies and evil of satan and move toward you. Let them read their Bibles, not to try to support evil but to try to find You, Lord. Help them Lord to see the truth that all Americans are indeed African Americans because you Lord began creation there. The Bible and science both agree that man's origins began in Africa. As you leave warmer climates for colder ones, melanin activation decreases, and the darker hues become lighter, but never will a "white" man ever exist because all our people of color range from the lightest pink to the darkest brown. Still all are people of color. Knowing the truth can be freeing. If the so called "white supremacists" win the next war that they are diligently trying to start, then they will enact DNA testing because of the false belief that there is a race of white people. If any portion, even 1%, shows African background then most people will again be categorized as something other than white, which no one is anyway.

What a mess we have made trying to gain the world and reaping the whirlwind. Man must come to his senses. The truth is well-known. Let's repent of the truth rather than continuing to hide it in order to hide from it. For hiding it is lying and only satan can be behind it. When you serve satan by your actions, God sees all and though you can fool man, you can never fool our God. You are found out and will be held to account for the evil perpetuated throughout your life. Repentance is yours and God is patient, but he demands a reckoning (Selah)

My heart breaks for the hued and hueloss who think they are serving God by their negativity and even lies to those who believe differently. It's funny how Social Security and Medicare are not socialism, yet government money to help with childcare is. People may not realize just how much childcare costs. Childcare payments today are often more than an average mortgage payment, but when the burden of such is not upon you, you don't have to recognize the truth of that burden. Think about what you would be denied if you had to handle such a financial burden with only two children; you could easily be paying more than $2000 monthly. That's $2000 not going into your retirement account, not going into savings for children's college, not going into a mortgage to build wealth for generations, and not being able to experience so many advantages of travel and life enhancing experiences for yourself and your children.

We need to begin to think more about others and the plight they face, rather than falsely thinking that help to others diminishes us. One thing in life is certain, we can never beat God's giving. All that God has for us will be ours, no matter how much we give out. Remember when Cain asked God if he was his brother's keeper, he was really expressing that God was not to hold him responsible for his brother. Yet God sent him away as punishment, as much for the attitude of selfishness as for the murder. It was selfishness that led America to enslave people of hue and advanced a lie that those who had hueloss were somehow gifted by God to denigrate people to a life of servitude to them.

Think about what came about because of our original sin from which we have yet to repent. The enslavers even made slaves use incest to increase their wealth. Enslaved hued men had to sleep with their sisters, mothers, aunts, daughters, etc. to make more slaves for the enslavers to increase his wealth. Many of the hueloss families are dealing with incest today because of it being fostered on the enslaved. They in turn did it within their own families also. Of course, it also continued among the freed enslaved as well as among the enslavers., Think about the destruction that it created in the freed enslaved and in the enslavers' families. Another generational curse created from selfish motives. The freed enslaved were still enslaved to a demented way of life with incest the norm in many families taking generations to get beyond a way of life that had been forced on them from the economic value of the hueloss. The hueloss are still using religion to hide behind as they do their evil. But more and more preachers are being exposed for the shameful acts imposed on the innocent.

So much of the ills of our society being blamed on those with hue have been set in motion by the hueloss, not out of hatred but simply out of greed. Putting drugs into a community to diminish it from within while creating wealth for those without is one of the greatest crimes in America. This was done by those of great wealth who will never pay the price of their deviance. Look at our modern-day tech industry. Young girls on display that men used to get their jollies, yet it doesn't stop there. They then go home and subject their daughters to what has been inflamed online. Too much America, too much. A day of reckoning is approaching, we must repent (Selah)

Joel 1:14 "Declare a holy fast, call a sacred assembly; summon the elders and all who live in the land to the House of the Lord your God and cry out to the Lord." 2:12 "Even now" declares the Lord, "return to me with all your heart with fasting and weeping and mourning." 13b "Return To the Lord your God, for He is gracious and compassionate, slow to anger and abounding in love, and He relents from sending calamity." America, we need to declare a holy fast, calling for a sacred assembly so that we can make an earnest attempt to go to the Lord with our whole hearts repenting of our original sin of the greed for money. We have used so many evil ways to obtain it, thinking that it was our god; yet knowing that God has called us to a higher place in Him. When we looked at our constitution and the amendments that have been made to it, you can tell that the call of God has always been there, yet we have too often gone the way of evil after the call of satan for greed and selfishness. Even now, some are trying to change the Constitution to adhere only to its original form and function, though it was designed to be a living breathing and changing document. Only God could have ordered men's minds to create such.

33

To make a people subhuman so you can justify use and abuse is not God but is certainly satan. To wrap it in God's permission and authority makes it even more satanic. How our Lord must grieve at what we have done and are now doing. What he meant for good in this country, we have used for evil. We are now at the point where we call good evil and evil good. Getting people to follow conspiracy theories that you know are lies because they make you lots of money, so you justify such evil. Remember the deaths of over 6,000 because you told lies is blood on your hands. This was not just the leaders but all the followers as well. The followers of governors who mandated death by disallowing masks and vaccine mandates surely have blood on their hands.

The QAnon liar who continues subverting the minds of people as he continues laughing at how foolish they are to resort to taking the lives of their own children who they had given life. How horrible it will be when they recognize that they have all been used and are being used for someone's selfish gain. When you wake up to the evil that you've caused in this country no amount of self-denial or self-indulgence will allow you to forget or forgive yourself of the horrors of what you've done. Deliberately dividing the country for your benefit of evil. Mary Trump says that her uncle is one who believes that it's never enough. He is said to laugh at those religious ones who gave him so much support, yet out of sight he mocked them. The lies to overturn a just election so that he doesn't have to pay the price of his misdeeds brought about January 6, 2021 that some compared to 9/11 and found January 6th to be worse.

Some were offended by the comparison, yet I can fully understand. 9/11 was done by foreigners, but January 6th was done by our own people who've been raised in this republic democracy yet tried to overthrow it. Continuing in the lies of hostility brings about more and more division that "white supremacists" (what a joke) are storing up for another civil war that they will once again lose. Fools fall for anything and its only fools who follow satan, calling it religion. Even preachers have been used to preach the evil to support someone's lies to keep them from paying the price of years of cheating, years of lying, years of other falsehoods to support a name brand that can make money. People thought they were getting a businessman. He promised to run America as he had done with his businesses. He did just that, for America is a failed state that may take generations to balance out again.

How horrible it will be if they refuse the repentance offered by God. Repentance should not be in secret, for the people must know. They will see blood on their hands, no matter how much they wash them. The whole lot of enablers will carry the blood of the lives lost on their hands and in their hearts, until repentance or an ugly death. It's time, America, to change the course of our history from evil to God. America has never been a Christian nation as shown by the evil constructs put in place for wealthy gain. But we can indeed try to be one now. It's not too late if we begin.

Pitting people one against another to make one group feel good about themselves is abhorrent. It's amazing that truth is now viewed as evil and so many condone refuting the truth to make some feel good about themselves. If I must lie to you in order for you to feel good, then you are simply living a lie. Whose child are you when you seek to serve lies? Satan is the honest answer. Ask yourself if you are content being the seed of satan. Or do you, as you vocally profess, want to be a child of God? God allows you to walk in truth, to feel bad about that truth, yet gives you a chance to repent of that truth.

The lies that America is living in at present will bring about our demise quicker than God intended. For He is long suffering and desires that our hearts and minds can be turned to Him, but His long suffering is not forever. How sad if we hold onto the lies because we don't have the fortitude of character to embrace the truth, be repulsed by that truth, and seek repentance from a God who loves us, rather than continuing following those who hate us by virtue of the lies they continue to spew to get money from us. When will we open our minds and hearts to seek truth so that we can walk in the truth that God desires, rather than the lies of satan. Choose you this day who you will serve. (Selah)

34

What will God say to those who have been taught that they only had to be against death of babies in the womb, go to a church house on Sunday or Saturday, support any Republican agenda in order to be Christians? They haven't become Christians even with submersion baptism. They went in dry devils and came out wet devils. So, what will He say? "Depart from me to the lake of fire for your wickedness." Your argument will be "but that's what we were taught to do." His response then will be, "but I told you in the word to study to show yourself approved." You chose not to study for the truth, but instead you just use the Bible to support what you chose to believe. You were against abortion, but you were for all the other ways of killing people of color. The killing by police was justified by saying "if they would just comply right away, they wouldn't get killed." They had to run because they don't want to be killed. So now the police are allowed to shoot them in the back, without having to pay for that crime.

You fight against pollution in your communities when they give notice that such is coming. No such notice is given in black and brown communities, so those deadly chemicals that sicken and kill are placed there. You put drugs in the same communities, knowing that if you can get them addicted, they will commit crime to foster your self-fulfilling prophecy, "they are just criminals anyway." It amazes me the lengths to which you will go to fulfill your false beliefs. Additionally, so many of the things afforded to the hueloss are absent for those who still have their hue. Romans 1:25-"They exchanged the truth about God for a lie and worshipped and served their creature rather than their Creator. That is where we are, America, and have been from its inception. The creature is money and the power obtained by creating a false teaching of "races", "intelligence", and "good and evil". That which is evil you call good now, though you know the deeds are evil.

Races don't exist. God created one race, "man," the human race. Male and female. He created them, not man and woman. Adam called Eve "woman", not God. God called her man, female man. We all began in Africa, whether hued still or hueloss; so how can you claim supremacy from what you've lost , which is most of your hue? It would make more sense to claim supremacy from gain not loss. Maybe you already know in your heart of hearts that you have lost something rather than gained an artificial supremacy. Maybe that is why you hate those who maintain their hue because you know it is strength and you have to denigrate that God-given strength and turn it into weakness. How pitiful! The color of a man's body is not his strength. The love in a man's heart is his true strength from God. Hate diminishes, love empowers. Do you see that distinction? Is It really hate or is it jealousy because you know the truth and had to manufacture a lie to the extent to cover up that truth? Your hatred has diminished you, oh hueloss one. It has not exalted you and never will.

You claim God's anointing, yet it is self-anointing on a satanic basis, not God's basis. God's basis is love, always has been and always will be. Anything else, we should know is a lie from men, not men of God, but men that follow satan rather than God. God had to create Eve man because she would be the one to express the love of God to the world. Amos 5:10 There are those who hate the one who upholds justice in court and detests the one who tells the truth. If the women of America didn't know God enough to recognize evil from God, they would instead of a godly man, elect a demon once again.

Man has from the beginning of time blamed the woman for the fall from grace. Preachers take great delight in preaching that men must be in control because Eve ate the forbidden fruit. Of course, we don't even know what she ate but it makes a neatly wrapped lie with little truth. God gave the command to Adam, not Eve and though Eve shouldn't have been tempted by satan's lies, it was Adam that sinned against God. Eve sinned against Adam, but Adam in partaking of what she had sinned against God. Men have used that to dominate the world, even though we are charged to take care of the world. Man in his evil need to have dominion, needed to dominate not because of actual need, but purely because of greed.

Twisting things from the Bible has often been man's way of justifying the evil done. The claim that God cursed black and brown people because of African heritage is a lie from the pit of hell that hueloss men choose to follow in order to justify their treatment of people of color. God cursed Canaan, not Ham from which many believe that people of color came from. Yet the truth is that we were all people of color at one time and the migration to colder, less sunny environments caused the lack of melanin activation leading to the loss of color. Look at toast, the higher and longer in the heat, the darker it gets. Just the opposite happens with mankind. All dark at first then migration created loss. If Africans were cursed, then we are all cursed.

The natural resources that are esteemed around the world occur naturally in Africa. The hueloss valued what these natural resources could bring them, so they found ways to exploit and steal them for their own benefit. By subjugating the people even in their original continents/countries, they were able to obtain those resources. Though from Europe and the U.S., hueloss people felt they had a right to all the riches in Africa or at least they laid claim to such. Greed of man has justified much evil and man's need to justify some God-given advantage has led to even more evil. Satan is the father of lies and liars and God always has the last word on all actions.

35

Time is running out given this pandemic. You may be the very next one to succumb to COVID, even while thinking that your hueloss gives you protection without a vaccine. It is ludicrous to think that your DNA is so advanced that you are naturally protected. Yes, you saw the hued people have devastation at their door. You forget that you set the social conditions that cause them to succumb more easily to it initially. Forced poverty in the U.S. and Brazil had more to do with it than skin color (Selah). Amos 5:18- "Woe to you who long for the day of the Lord. Why do you long for the day of the Lord? That day will be darkness, not light." This serves as a warning to those who claim to love the Lord yet hate His people, for what you expect to receive is just the opposite of your just reward. For you have denied justice to God's people that He directed you to care for. Rather than care for them, you, instead exploited them at every turn. You even used the courts to side with your evil against justice, rather than for justice.

You spend hours trying to figure out the date that Jesus returns for His people, yet if you were truly one of His, that date would matter not. Expecting to go to glory and arriving in hell as you deserve will be a far different experience than you expected. There you will finally come to the full knowledge of what you have been and are. It will be too late to repent then, so once again I beg you to seek the Lord with your whole heart and live a life that honors God rather than one that he despises.

How are you able to justify to God your evil against others? You can't, simply because He has placed a seed of Himself in every man that you had to cast out to receive the evil that you've been walking in. Ignorance will not be an excuse, for you were given a choice. You were free to choose who you would serve and you, against all principles, chose satan because he answered the desires of privilege that were not yours, but was stolen from others. It's amazing how you have tried to justify your evil to self and others, even those who suffer from your injustice. Are all people but you and your kind fools that they will believe the lies that fall so easily from your lips, having imparted from a satanic-filled heart?

The day of reckoning draws nigh, pray God's mercy to put it off, for you are far from ready. He in His great compassion has put it off, hoping that you would come to the full knowledge of Him and therefore yourself. For if you never recognize your evil then you will continue the justification of withholding justice from others. Your greed is like a magnet, drawing all things to yourself, never realizing that man needs to earn a decent wage to care for his/her family, and instead of great wealth for yourself, paying a decent wage will not put you in poverty. We have veterans sleeping in the streets of America and yet have those who don't even want to pay $15 an hour for honest work. This, while you are worth billions that won't save you in the end. You can build hundreds of bunkers that won't give you any protection from the wrath of God (Selah) Obadiah 1:3- "The Pride of your heart has deceived you, you who live in the clefts of the rocks and make your home on the heights.: When you live in lofty places with your vast wealth it becomes easier to think that God has blessed you to live in such a way, yet the time will come when you beg for help. Some hueloss people are now even refusing help from nurses and doctors of color and are given reinforcements of that evil by being given accommodations by the hospital administrators. These are the very people who thought in error that only black and brown people would be devastated by COVID, yet they too of the lofty places are now succumbing to this deadly virus. It was allowed to run rampant to bring death to those you viewed as inferior, killing over 6000 people initially. Now those same lofty ones, not by income but by their self-proclaimed DNA, are refusing to get vaccines for COVID; yet are willing to use medication meant for animals that they believe will heal

151

COVID. How stupid do you have to be to believe this? About as stupid as so many claimed to believe the lie that the 2020 election was stolen. It didn't have to be stolen after so many people defected from the Republican running for another turn.

They counted on the evil of the hueloss to make him a king to serve for life. Serve is used wrongfully here. He only served himself. He never wanted to be president because presidents must work, and you can easily see by all of his failed businesses that he must not like to work. Being a con man was his natural ability, but conning family is one thing, while conning a nation quite another. Democrats weren't involved in counting or certifying the votes in those states where they claim the votes were stolen. Do you really believe that he ever even cared for you, those of you who stormed the capital trying to stop the certification's final process? He didn't then and doesn't now. He is only using you in hopes that you will be stupid enough to start a civil war based on his lie. He has now told you to protest mightily if he is indicted, but I pray you will have enough sense not to do so.

36

Look at reality, if you start that war and create a totalitarian government with him as the head, he will not want any association with you. He has already said that you make him look bad. He didn't know that you were such lost souls that would continue to believe his and his henchman's lies to keep following him. You give him your money so he can continue to live among the rich. He will never stop grifting you. Even when he goes to jail, you will be sending him funds because he has mesmerized you. You call him a straight talker and straight shooter. He is neither. He is a certified con man who has made some of you so mentally disturbed that you have done things that you never thought you would do. Our democracy only works by the powers of the people. If you give that democracy away, you no longer have one.

He said, "to fight hard or you'll have no more country." I say fight hard for democracy by walking away from the lies so that you will keep your country. He hates you because you have not amassed wealth and power like he has. You chose not to lie and cheat at every turn, but that was not his choice. Wake up from preachers who are leading you to satan and listen to your mighty God who gives you chance after chance to come to repentance. One day it may be too late, but today you have a chance to turn things around. Carrying the flag of the Christian Church in no way will make you a Christian. You must learn the thinking and behavior of a Christian to be a follower of Christ.

Get a Bible with the words of Jesus in red so you can find out before it's too late! Jonah 2:8- Those who cling to worthless idols turn away from God's love for them. We often want God to forgive us for the evil we do, but not others who we in our pride try to believe don't deserve to be forgiven. When Jesus died on that cross, it wasn't just for me, but for all mankind who would choose to believe on and to follow Him. We need to pray for all and recognize that their evil is no different from ours. The greatest sins can be forgiven by a great God. We need to always pray for God's heart towards others and that's one of the purposes of the church. It's so sad that we don't even recognize the idols that we cling to. Perhaps we don't realize that if we have an idol, we've automatically turned from God.

God has asked us time and time again to have no other gods before Him or in competition with Him. Our lack of faith in the one, the true God, is the reason we turn to idols so easily. To make man an idol is an undue burden, not just for you, but for him too. That man can do nothing but fail. One wrong word and they are exposed. An admission that they took a vaccine after playing down the severity of COVID was the beginning of the end. The one truth that was told got him pushed off the pedestal of idol worship. I wait in promise to see how God, not man, will retrieve His throne. Church people really created the idol because the one true God was not enough for them. The sin of idolatry can be forgiven but those seeking forgiveness must have some level of actual recognition of sin and then remorse for that sin.

Some people just ask God to forgive then without confession of anything because they never come into true confession or understanding of their sin. They tend to believe that if they just ask for forgiveness each day without specificity of the action, God must forgive them. God is not a genie who operates to give us our desires. God demands repentance. How does one repent of that which they know not is sin? They don't. They depend on religion which has led far more people to hell than any sinful lifestyle has done. God hates religion.

To keep religious rules, yet they neglect all that God's word tells us we are to do in order to be a Christian may fool man, but never God. A Christian's heart does God things automatically, yet a religious heart sticks to the minimum requirements of rule keeping. Christians see a God that's bigger than any problem while religion looks to someone to blame for any problem. Religion may overtly teach the evils of racism though they know that God created but one race, the human race. He created man, male and female He created them.

Men unfortunately have taken God's creation to dominate rather than take care of. He dominates women to make himself seem greater than he is. He kills animals for sport, not food. He demands to be better and do better than others. Even changing laws to operate in his lust-filled needs. Remember, lust is not just confined to sex. Watch the behavior of our so-called politicians. It doesn't matter which side they ascribed to; they mostly are doing what brings them personal wealth, often at our expense. This too is religious teaching that our Lord hates. What will a man gain when he gives up his soul for coins, even for coins in the billions? He gives up a right relationship with a God who demands righteousness (Selah)

Have we counted the cost of giving up our relationship with God for a counterfeit relationship with man? If we count the cost, we may find that the cost of a temporary relationship with man is the cost of eternal life with a loving, forgiving and just God. We say we seek eternity with Him, but our demonic beliefs and behaviors show that to be a lie. How can I not love many hued brothers and sisters and expect God to love me? We count him a lie if that is our expectation. Jesus words in red tell us what he expects from us. Though we don't have to give the other cheek when we've been slapped, he is truly expecting us to forgive. Sometimes that forgiveness still demands separation for safety's sake, yet we still must do so.

37

So often we don't know why things happen as they do but we can take everything in our lives as a learning experience with our God. As we learn to forgive and to rest in the Lord, we draw ever closer to Him. He, on far too many occasions, has had to forgive us for our deeds of corruption. Our deeds of corruption have been to think that we are better than another, that we are more deserving of privilege than another, that God has ordained us to rule over others, or that our way of thinking is the right way, even if the word of God that we proclaim is not His word at all. This has led to a demented way of thinking and has so corrupted our society that we won't get vaccines to the detriment of little children. Yet, here again we say we are pro-life when the absence of mask and vaccines readily show us as pro death.

Even the preachers are so beguiled in deception that they tell you Jesus will keep you from getting the virus because of your privilege with Him. God doesn't want us to be fools, yet we show Him that it is our preference. And we don't have to think of others at all. After all, we can't allow a political position unlike ours to be successful and instead must allow every manipulative satanic message to be our guide for redress and address. Sadly, it may take seeing your children or other loved ones die because you made the wrong choice before you will come out from the demonic influence of evil. When you watch your children die and those leaders tell you it was somehow the will of God, wake up at least to recognize that you are the murderer not the virus or other people.

Seek the Kingdom of God and He will give you the answers you need to be safe in a climate of danger from the virus, safe from the lunatics who are in Congress, safe from the wealthy who push getting the virus and using other drugs to keep you from dying even though those things wouldn't be needed if you took the vaccines and wore a mask. The United States has lost its mission of union that stands for" united". We are always to think of the common good rather than self. We are to love the wonderful mixture that we are, rather than to esteem one and demean another. We are to believe that as citizens we share the same rights. Never can one vote of a person reduce the value of others as you were told by media personalities. Though born in racism, God has designed us to move away from that because He knows that He created one race, the human race which is man, male and female. Adam wasn't better coming from dirt than Eve coming from Adam. The foolishness of how we think has really been exposed during this pandemic and instead of standing with decreasing it by using safety measures, you stood with lies and foolishness for which you and yours will pay. (Selah)

Micah 6:7b -"Will I offer my firstborn for my transgressions, the fruit of my body for the sin of my soul?" 8-"He has shown you, O mortal, what is good and what does the Lord require of you?" To act justly and to love mercy and to walk humbly with your God. Some are actually allowing their children to die from COVID and killing other people's children too. The transgressions of your heart and mind to try to live any way you desire rather than to follow the recommendations of doctors to fight this pandemic has led to foolish behaviors from foolish thinking. Others see how foolish you've become and foster more foolishness for their purpose.

The United States will not have another civil war, though in your foolishness you are trying to incite such. Is a person leading you really worthy of you losing your soul? You are soul sick, but there is a cure. Believe on the Lord so that He can turn your mind to right-thinking. If you feed on evil, all that your soul can desire is more evil. Those of you hueloss who claim to have built this country operate on a lie. The first of many lies. The enslaved and other minorities built this country and no one else should claim otherwise. It's time to know the truth and time to start telling the truth. Your children need to operate in truth, or we will have no country. You would destroy it to maintain a lie.

Even now the African Americans, Latin Americans, Asian Americans, and Native Americans built this country. You created laws to allow you to control what others created. How many of you will grow and pick crops for you to eat? How many of you will work in the slaughterhouses of the U.S.? How many of you are willing to take care of the trash? Far too few, I know. How working in the fields all day? The U.S. would dissolve because of the factions. The hueloss poor against the hueloss wealth of America. You know who would win. You can't devise enough evil to win against greed and selfishness.

Right now, you are soul sick and the only way out of it is repentance. No other option is available. Stop believing lies so that the truth can penetrate your brain and body. Our time may be short! What does the Lord require- to act justly and to love mercy and to walk humbly with your God. Ask yourself, "have I done this by....?" You can't answer in the affirmative because your mind has been further warped by so many conspiracy theories which aren't theories at all.

Critical race theory is a true theory no matter how we might object to the truth of it. It's simply a construct that lays bare the truth of America. It doesn't have to remain our truth for our Lord is granting us time to change things. If we just simply hide truth and choose to continue living in lies, we remain lost. QAnon is a conspiracy theory devised to get you to hate Democrats. Why do they desire such? Is it because they believe in sharing the wealth rather than creating laws for the rich to gain more? The ones who devised that conspiracy theory are the ones who are peddling children for sex, not Hillary Clinton. Foolish thinking to the point that people have died because of your choosing to believe lies, which shows that God is absent from your life and satan is in full control.

We have not acted justly towards others and deny our privilege. Hueloss persons in poverty are being pitted against the persons of hue by the hueloss persons of wealth. Why do you think this is? They use you to keep them in wealth and to help them gain more wealth and power. You will always be the loser, even if no person of color exists. Who do you think will have to work for little or no wage? You will be the one. Class systems will keep you from gaining. No more colorism, yet classism will keep you down. After they use you to oppress those of color, until they all leave the U.S., you will be the poor and downtrodden. This will be your reality. You are being used to give what little you have now to ones who only want more wealth and power. Though you gave a certain amount, you were charged far more so that they could use you to maintain a lie.

Never using their own funds or even the money that was gained from you by lies and deceit, only used to make them richer. More money, more power is the name of the game. Don't think you will be exempt. You make claims of "pro-life", yet it is only "pro womb". And you think that is laudable. Unbelievable that your density of heart and mind can't reveal truth to yourself. You stay in deception because of your evil thinking. No one can keep you in stupidity but you. Come out from that and learn to love once again. The enemy is not people of color but the wealthy in power who want not to share the wealth but want to control the wealth to maintain their power. Keeping you foolish is how they continue to do it (Selah)

Nahum 1:3- "The lord is slow to anger but great power; the Lord will not leave the guilty unpunished." Though the guilty will not go unpunished, God is slow to anger but quick to forgive. It's time to heal America and we all must be part of that healing process. First recognize the truth that Trump really did lose the presidential race of 2020. That has been the most recent catalyst of ignorant and foolish behavior. When you recognize the truth ask all of those who you've hurt by your thuggish behavior for forgiveness. Recognize that the calamity you brought to our country can only be healed by you. Trying to make hued people the racists, villains and even antifa only compounds the problems that were started.

Trump may never admit the truth because he won't be able to grift you anymore if he does. He wanted more wealth and power and used the foolish ones of our country and the world to try to gain it. Thank God for the women who were able to see truth. For to see truth is to see God. We must see God and hear from Him. If you remain full of satan there can be no room for God because satan won't allow it. He has devised a plan to keep you all to himself, knowing that it leads to your eternal demise. Remember he does not want to be in hell alone. You need to hold Trump and all those political, religious, and other leaders responsible for the state of our country with its present divisiveness.

Fox News and lesser-known media companies must be sued to pay the price of January 6, 2021, and even the resultant costs after that. How dare men go to a female principal with zip ties because she expected their child to quarantine after exposure to Covid. This has been a principle in place to try to halt the spread of this virus. So many lies have spread regarding Dr. Fauci, endangering his life and his family. How do you justify what you did to an innocent man who was trying to save your life? DeSantis, one of the guilty parties, leading your children to death to gain a few coins which leads to more power. All those governors who mandated no mask and no vaccines will have a special place in hell because every death can be attributed to their leadership.

My heart grieves for them because they have lost all moral compass. Remember they weren't killing their own children with their ruling; they were killing yours. Repentance is the first thing yet if we know not that we've sinned, it doesn't happen. God desires that we recognize and grieve our sin before we confess. For confession of the mouth is no confession unless it involves the heart and head in recognition of our sin. God is a holy God, not to be reckoned with. He is as holy as He is loving and expects the same from us.

America, we must awaken to this truth. We've been duped by people for their own malicious purposes and if we remain blind to their evil, we will be no more. Don't keep hating your neighbor for crooks. For that is exactly what they are. You really got caught up in a tsunami of evil. Television media, Facebook and others surged with money, which justified more evil. New reports from Facebook shows that traffic for lies was six times the traffic for truth. If they had shut that down, how many lives may have been saved? Facebook is a good thing, but it can be and is being used by the unscrupulous just to make them wealth. Wealth equals power, yet when you sell your soul, no amount of money will be satisfactory. It will be an always striving and driving endeavor that keeps you out of control and out of the will of our Lord.

My heart is heavy with the realization of what some Republican governors have done not just in regard to COVID, but even in the electrical grid system. God has shown us the truth though we have refused to see it and charge those responsible. It's reprehensible that politicians have gotten away with the evil they've done to the point of causing death by policy. Why would you want a person to get monoclonal therapy after getting the plague, rather than getting the much cheaper vaccine and wear a mask? Only because your pockets are being enlarged as you enlarge your benefactor(s) pockets.

Oh, for shame that you will kill a child out of utero, yet claim you are pro-life for a fetus not yet out into the world. You are truly a lie. For if you are willing to kill children out of bodies by your laws and mandates, they would have been better off not to make it out of the womb. You have suffered the little children that Jesus said to "suffer not". How do you condone your divided way of thinking? Truly you don't! Pro-life is a nice thing to say because it only causes you to be against something that's none of your business. yet when you're called on to be for something that actually saves lives but will cost money now, you're against it all. Free lunch for the hungry children may cause them to become spoiled you say, and you claim the same for a living wage for a mother or father so they can work only one job might give their child a leg up and allow them to be competitive in academics and in business. You may fool yourself, but you will never fool our God. He sits high yet looks low and sees all (Selah).

2Peter 2:1-3, 9-10, 21; 2 Peter 1:5-7 -It's time to heal America! Become a part of the healing process. First recognize that there are false prophets among the people, just as there are false teachers among you. They will secretly introduce destructive heresies (conspiracies). Many will follow their depraved conduct and will bring the way of truth into dispute. In their greed they will exploit you with fabricated stories. The Lord knows how to rescue the godly from trials and to hold the unrighteous for punishment. This is especially true for those who follow the corrupt desire of the flesh and despise authority.

It would have been better had you never known the way of righteousness than to turn your backs on the sacred commands that were passed on to you. Make every effort to add to your faith-goodness, knowledge, self-control, perseverance, godliness, mutual affection, and love. God provides the script for our lives in His word, yet the very ones who so vocally claim Him deny Him by their very actions. God created man in Africa--all man, male and female - He created them. From the dirt He formed Adam as a man of color and from Adam, God took Eve as the first woman of color; so understand that no one is white! They are just hueloss people. Hueloss because their color has been diminished by the deactivation of their melanin with which they are still born.

Remember you will never be hueless because that's how you get the tan by reactivating your melanin. The Bible and science both show this truth that man may try to refute, yet it remains the truth. Well, if no one is white, then there can be no white supremacy, for we are all cousins. Family, even cousins, look out for each other, not tear each other down with malicious treatment. Don't claim an advantage that you only gained from satan for it will only be shown in the end to have been a lie. Instead claim every advantage of love and clear thinking that God has given us. Pray about everything that you read on social media, understanding that the more salacious they can make their pronouncements, the more money they make, and the more satan will have it passed on.

39

My heart aches that we've let so many take advantage to divide our country, based on a lie or lies. Ask God to help you discern truth so you can walk away from lies. A past president will not be reinstated as president and the present president will never turn over the White House to a previous one unless it is by the votes of the people in the next election. Recognize that a report of the Arizona audit (false audit) will never be given as truth because it made far too much money for those who sell it as truth. The claim that black people hate America because they turn away from the flag and don't like the National Anthem is a lie. Those people are simply trying to bring attention to the racism that appears to persuade every law or rule made in America. If they didn't love America, they would no longer be here.

There are countries that are more welcoming and offer a cheaper cost of living than America. Try to think beyond your evil teachings. To withhold the truth of the horrors of slavery and our racist past and present doesn't keep any decent person from knowing the truth and hating the truth. The children won't feel bad about truth, they feel bad about the lies. Let them know the truth so they can gain a better understanding of their cousins of many hues.

We have done misdeeds to many groups of people, though none so dastardly as the African American that were raped and bred within families and by the enslavers just to produce more babies for slavery to bring wealth to the enslavers and the country. America lost its soul to gain that wealth. We must regain it and we can, but only with truth. God desires that we walk in truth. If the truth is hurtful to you who perpetuated the racism, know that it was doubly hurtful and harmful to the ones on whom it was inflicted. Let us awaken to a truth that compels us to repentance and a positive change. Look at the Statue of Liberty and the chains that have fallen at her feet. This shows that liberty for any man can only be had when there is liberty for all men. If you believe yourself to be supreme then you are in competition with God, not man, not a man that you believe to be your inferior.

For the love of God, we must change; otherwise we will meet a horrendous end that could easily be avoided simply by a spirit of repentance and a change in laws and attitudes. Replacement theory is out the window because no one can replace you. So, stop believing this nonsense. The desire is not to replace you. People use this to provoke fear and bring forth more evil deeds. If you stopped giving money to the likes of those who espouse those lies, then they would quickly turn to another theory to promote fear for the sole purpose of getting wealth.

Wealth's equality with power has been the driving force in our country for far too long. God must become our driving force. In any church or ministry that claims Christ but doesn't obey Christ is just heresy. Demand repentance, a time for fasting and seeking God's face so that America can achieve the greatness that we are known by others can become our truth within. Hiding truth from generation to generation only exacerbates the evil thinking and doing, from generation to generation. Remember, the evil one can only exist and keep expanding because of you. Truth, though it may be embarrassing, may cause some pain because it's not easy to see the negative truth of those we love; but true love needs truth to really be love. Rather than loving an image, we can truly love a person. God doesn't pretend that we are anything or anyone other than who we are. We who belong to Him can love like He does - the truth of who you are even though that truth shows clearly the evil of your heart. That's how we can love the person, not just the false images of the person.

Satan is the only one who would have you lie about America's past, time after time. He likes to be hidden from truth. Understand that he is the one behind this division, not God. Zechariah 1:2b- "Return to me declares the Lord almighty and I will return to you says the Lord almighty." His word is one that is entrusted to us and can be depended on. Given all the evil that we've boasted of and all the evil we did to gain prominence in the world, He will show us that much of it has been evil and we have much to repent of. If we hope to continue existing, we must repent. There is no other option.

Obadiah 1:4-"Though you soar and exalt yourself as an eagle and nest among the stars, still I will bring you down, declares the Lord." Your placement of yourself on the heights is not sustainable, for God sits higher than the stars above the eagles and sees all that you do. Moreover, He alone knows that evil of your heart and the true motivations of your actions. Don't fool yourself that because He has patiently waited for you to seek truth that He may continue to wait. Repentance is our only way out of the massive evil that we've created in America. Obadiah 1:15-Tells us that the day of the Lord is near for all nations. "As you have done, it will be done to you; your deeds will return upon your own head."

40

epentance never comes from fear but from a truly contrite
heart. We can only get that contrite heart through truth. Feel the
full measure of the evil that you fostered upon others and know in your
heart of hearts to call it sin. Whenever we are out of the will of God, it
is indeed sin. Even if fleetingly in our conscious, it is sin. But you've
made a practice of your evil that has lasted many lifetimes. Your claim
to be pro-life is sin because it is just used as a rallying cry to draw
people to you, even though they see all the evil you do. If you were
pro-life, you would want things for others that foster a positive life for
children. Schools would be as well-equipped in the ghettos of
America as in the wealthiest suburbs. Daycare would be provided
based on income so people wouldn't have to work 2 or 3 jobs to make
ends meet. There would be fairness in medical needs, fairness in
decent housing, fairness in living a quality life and passing on a life of
quality for generations. The toxic chemicals that impact the air and
water would not only be in poor or minority communities as is done
now.

So much would change if we were really trying to be ready for repentance. Putting a band-aid on the truth or outright denying the truth will never lead to repentance. Repentance comes from a mind change that is led by a heart change. If you are the beneficiary of any change enacted, it's never repentance. You've just found another clever way to take advantage of others to benefit self. We are asked by God to look out for each other while we are on the earth, yet we seem to only look out for ourselves. Even you preachers are no better than and often worse than those who attend with listening ears and hearts. The word of God has been so subverted in your mind that you can only preach an adulterated word to the congregation. You have fostered division for your own evil gains. First, teaching what the slave owners told you to preach. Even using what was called the "Slave Bible" which is still housed at the Bible Museum in Washington, DC.

Today you are still doing the same. The wealthy and powerful tell you what to preach so you can have and maintain a life of privilege that you've made yourself believing that you are owed. Remember your preached word is not the last word, for God will still speak and He is not saying the same things as you.

Zechariah 1:3b- "Return to me declares the Lord almighty and I will return to you." 4: b-Turn from your evil ways and your evil practices. You may ask, "what evil ways and evil practices?" Fear is the great evil way that leads to evil practices. For you saw with the first group of Africans to come to America that they were industrious, hardy, eager to learn and eager to please. The fear that gripped you caused you to follow the satanic lies of one being better than the other, even to the point of developing an artificial barometer such as intelligence testing, supremacy by hueloss, and wealth as a blessing from God. This further led to the lifetime delegation of a people with hue to enslavement and the stealing of many of their inventions as your own. So stolen wealth began the greatness of our nation and without repentance it will be its downfall.

It's not too late to change course because our Father is truly a loving, forgiving, and faithful God. He is willing to forgive the greatest sins, not just those you may consider minor. You make the claim of pro-life, yet do everything in amassing wealth to be pro-death. Your actions fall far short of your claims. But still, it's not too late. How many more must die due to your lies about an election, lies about persons, and lies about a pandemic and treatments for the same?

I pray that you see the blood on your hands for you have been a party to this. Our Father holds you even more responsible than most, because you have led a charge of lies and corruption; and that which you didn't lead, you supported and upheld for others. Where is your shame, you who claim to be Christians? You justify your hatred of a man because of his hue, yet you are the ones who lost your hue. Your forefathers had the same hue before migration to colder climates. Yet your loss, you count as an advantage and have developed our country to accept this lie of superiority. You've also fostered it on other countries around the world as Europe fostered it on you.

God sits high and sees all; and without repentance, the day of reckoning will fall mightily. It's time to awake from the dream you've been living and the nightmare that you have caused others to live because of your fear and your greed. These ramblings of hopeful insight presented here are simply intended to prick the hearts and minds of my brothers and sisters who claim Christ to turn things around in this country, our country, so that God doesn't have to send more drastic measures of His displeasure to us.

Repent my brothers, repent my sisters, repent the preachers, prophets, teachers of the Word. Repent those who fear loss and embrace one in love who still has hue. Hued ones embrace those who have suffered hueloss and forgive their iniquity as we desire God to forgive all. Repent, Repent, Repent!!

If your heart has been touched by our Lord by the truth spoken here, please join with me in a prayer of repentance:

Our Lord and our God, we come before you with a repentant heart. We now see how we, in not trusting You to provide, have led us to awful behavior toward ourselves and others. Our children are not upset with our past because we have never told the truth of that past. Let our hearts be heavy so that we can proclaim no more lying and no more covering things up. We have sinned so mightily with lies and hiding the truth that our children want no part of our churches because they are wise enough to know that we lie to them. They are dropping out of the churches, yet we blame others for that. They hear the evil that we proclaim against others which they know is a lie. In segregation, we were able to hide truth more easily, but the cover has been taken off now, so our children see us for what we are. Help us repent before them and begin teaching them what you, Lord, teach us in your word. Not the changed word that has made race refer to people groups, but that which shows it was a contest.

If you Lord had created races of people, we would not have had to wait until recent years to see it in your Word. Help us honor all people that you created, for we are all created in your image and desire your heart, Lord. Help us change. We know it won't be easy, but we are now willing to learn and look at the truth of the lies that we have been living. Lord, help us help our children who have turned to drugs because we have made their lives so toxic. Help us learn to deal with them in truth and honesty from this point on. Help me to recognize my privilege in the laws of America and help me lend a hand to those who I witness lack privilege. Father God, please let me see and grieve all the evil that I have been, so that I can go deeply into repentance with you. Lord, we need you desperately. This is your country and I pray to become a part of its healing, rather than continuing in its demise. Hear our prayer, Oh 'Lord and lead us to your very heart so that we can only operate henceforth in your will.

CPSIA information can be obtained
at www.ICGtesting.com
Printed in the USA
LVHW051608250522
719694LV00012B/1271